# AMENDMENT to the CONSTITUTION

## Averting the Decline and Fall of America

# James O. Pace

JOHNSON, PACE, SIMMONS, & FENNELL PUBLISHERS
Los Angeles 1986

AMENDMENT TO THE CONSTITUTION
Averting the Decline and Fall of America

For information address:

Johnson, Pace, Simmons & Fennell Publishers
P.O. Box 711207
Los Angeles, California 90071


First Printing 7,728
Second Printing


**Library of Congress Cataloging-in-Publication Data**
Pace, James O., 1954-
Amendment to the Constitution.
Includes bibliographical references and index
1. Population—Law and legislation—United States.
2. United States—Social conditions. 3. United States—Moral conditions. 4. United States—Race relations.
I. Title.
KF3771.P33 1985      344.73      85-14611


ISBN 0-9615268-0-7   347.304

# PREFACE

When the fate of a nation and a people is imperiled from within its own ranks, and from aliens who have joined its ranks, and when within the space of one or two generations, the society established by its forefathers has been riven from its frame, the guardians of that nation must take action to defend their people from their own destructive elements and repair their defects, or be held responsible before God and man for their inaction. America is such a nation; the 1980s are a part of such a generation and our local elected officials are the guardians of whom I speak.

The purpose of this text is to remind this generation of its obligations to its country, to enlighten it in some measure as to its defects and destructive elements, and to present a plan to correct them.

President Reagan said in his famous national television speech, "A Time for Choosing," delivered October 1964, "I am going to talk of controversial things. I make no apology for this."[1] I, too, will talk of controversial things and I will recommend action that is extreme and polemic. However, we live in extreme and polemic times, with division among ourselves more common than unity. Any action, therefore, but inaction, may be viewed by some to be extreme. Subjects discussed herein may be considered by some to be sensitive and even outrageous, but the incensed and outraged will be those who by their action or at times by their very presence within the nation were themselves outrageous and controversial twenty years ago.[2] The course of action recommended by this text is a constitutional amendment presented to the several states through a convention called by Congress upon petition by the several states through their legislatures as provided for in Article V of the Constitution. It is to these state legislatures, who would have the foremost responsibility for action, that this text is primarily directed.

The time for action is now. As President Reagan said, "You and I have a rendezvous with destiny. We can preserve for our children this last best hope of man on earth or we can sentence them to take the first step into a thousand years of darkness. If we fail, at least let our children and our children's children say of us we justified our brief moment here. We did all that could be done."[3]

# CONTENTS Page

**CONTENTS**

**CONTENTS** Page

# AMENDMENT to the CONSTITUTION

# I. TRENDS IN AMERICA

## 1. Introduction

America has changed dramatically in the last thirty years. Rapid and extreme change has affected every region of our country and every aspect of our lives. Advancements in such areas of natural science as chemistry, physics, agriculture, electronics and engineering have improved the quality of our lives, have made us healthier, and have given us more comforts. The opposite side of the advancements made in natural sciences are the changes that have occurred in the social sciences, in such areas as law, politics, religion, ethics, race relations and the structure of our society and activities of its members. Changes that have occurred in these areas are as profound and dramatic as the changes in the natural sciences. However, where changes made in the natural sciences can generally be called advancements, changes in the social sciences cannot be considered such.[4] Indeed, as we will examine below, the order and structure of our society is as marked by decline as world technology is marked by advancement.

In America's quest for a more progressive and better life, many of the advancements made in the area of technology are offset by regression in our social order and structure. And just as technological inferiority will result in defeat in the battlefield and in the marketplace at the hands of our enemies and competitors, social inferiority will result in our conquest by superior or more artfully structured social orders, or possibly by more primitive but more effective social orders, or demise by internal collapse.

In order to determine the current state of our society, let us briefly examine its various aspects and see what changes have recently occurred therein. We shall examine aspects of change in the context of two primary areas, racial identity and standards of conduct. Our racial identity encompasses such issues as racial composition and culture. Only racial composition, however, will be discussed herein. Our standards of conduct are divided into three categories, those concerning the family, those concerning the community and those concerning industry. The standards of conduct concern-

1

ing the family include such issues as living patterns and sexual ethics. The standards of conduct concerning the community include religion, crime, drug abuse, entertainment and litigation. Concerning industry, the standards of conduct include poverty, education, technology, and public works. A summary of recent changes in our society regarding these issues is set forth below.

## 2. Racial Identity

### (a) Racial Composition of the Nation

The statistics and facts relating to racial composition and demographics in America are incomplete in many respects. Two causes of this are (i) the undocumented and undocumentable illegal aliens in this nation, the numbers of which are impossible to calculate accurately, and (ii) the method of classification employed by government agencies, including the U.S. Bureau of the Census, which often obscures racial classification. No one knows how many illegal aliens are in America nor how many enter each year. The issue is sensitive and volatile. Liberal and minority groups cite low estimates while politically conservative groups cite higher figures.[5] Possibly the only way to get a real feeling as to the number of illegal aliens is to visit such states as Texas and California where the highest concentration of them reside[6] and observe the situation firsthand.

Incompleteness in facts relating to racial composition and demographics arises further because U.S. government agencies do not always compile statistics in a clear or consistent manner. The government records various statistics concerning Hispanics and Spanish-origin persons, but has not been uniform in its classification of them. At times, Hispanics have been classified as nonwhite, and at other times as white, and currently, they are not divided according to race at all. For example, in the various Fetal Death Ratio, Neonatal, Infant, and Maternal Mortality Rates by Race: 1915 to 1970, the Mexicans were at times included in the category "Negro and Other,"[7] and at other times were included in the category "White."[8] Mexicans did not change their skin color, but government statisticians changed their classification. Currently, the trend in U.S. government statistics is to include a footnote for data concerning Hispanics providing: "Persons of Spanish origin may be of any race."[9] The inconsistency of this is compounded by the rebuttable presumption that exists in the U.S. government to the effect that Hispanics are white,[10] which means, for example, that statistics regarding Mexicans are often combined with those for Anglo-Saxons. Further, in surveys for government purposes concerning matters of race, the current definition of white includes Middle Easterners and persons from Asia Minor as well as Europeans.[11] Thus, often for statistical purposes, Arabs and Anglo-Saxons are grouped together. For purposes of this text, Middle Easterners, persons from Asia Minor and Hispanics are generally not classified as white. With this state of affairs in mind, let us examine the racial composition of America yesterday and today.

In 1950, the population of the United States was just over 150 million, of which more than 135 million were white and about 15 million were non-white.[12] Hispanics, because of their small numbers, did not constitute a separate category. The American population was 90 percent white. In 1960, the population of the United States was just over 180 million, of which over 160 million were white, 19 million were Negroes, and 1.6 million were of other races. America was about 89 percent white and 11 percent Negro and other races.[13] The 1960 census did not generally contain separate categories for the Hispanics, Orientals, Pacific Islanders or other nonwhite groups. There were only three classifications: "white," "Negro" and "Other." Census takers were instructed to classify Hispanics as either "white" if their appearance was white or "Other" if their appearance was nonwhite.[14] Again, the documented Hispanic population constituted only a small percentage of the population so uniform statistics concerning them generally were not kept. Gradually the Hispanic immigration grew until the U.S. Census Bureau felt it was necessary to classify them separately. During the 1970s the documented Hispanic population increased by 61 percent.[15] "Between 1977 and 1978, huge increases of Vietnamese and Mexican immigrants accounted for 95 percent of the total rise in immigration."[16]

In 1980, the population of the United States was over 226 million[17] of which nonwhites, including Hispanics, totalled over 52 million.[18] In other words, by 1980, America had, of record, become 23 percent nonwhite. These figures do not include an accurate estimation of the undocumented illegal aliens (primarily Hispanic and Oriental) who number many millions more. The U.S. Immigration and Naturalization Service maintains accurate records of legal U.S. immigrants but, of course, has no accurate figures as to the number of illegal immigrants currently in the United States or the number entering each year. Based upon the number of illegal immigrants actually apprehended at the U.S. border by the Border Patrol, it is estimated that, in all, over 4 million Mexicans illegally immigrated to the United States in 1983 alone,[19] with only 1 million being apprehended. This does not include the Filipinos, the Taiwanese, the Central Americans, etc. who also illegally entered the United States in large numbers. It should be noted that permanent illegal white immigration to the United States constitutes a negligible percentage of the total illegal population.

It is impossible to estimate the number of illegal nonwhites in America who appear on no uniform government record. Our records do show for the last decade, however, the ratio of legal white immigration to legal nonwhite immigration. Comparing the race and nationality of legal immigrants arriving in the 1970s with those who came in the mid-1960s, the changing face of America becomes readily apparent. In the 1970s, 4.3 million immigrants were admitted by the Immigration and Naturalization Service into the United States. During this period, there were 4.6 percent fewer European immigrants than in the mid-1960s, and there were 815 percent more Asians.[20] Because of much higher fertility rates and mass immigration, the Mexican population alone has been doubling every ten years. In the last ten years, the Korean population has grown by 413 percent, the Filipinos by 126 percent and the Chinese population by 85 percent.[21]

From 1951 to 1960, about 1.8 million of the 2.5 million recorded immigrants came from Europe, Australia, New Zealand, Canada or other white countries,[22] comprising 72 percent of the total immigrants for this period. According to the U.S. Census, from 1971 to 1979, of the 4.6 million recorded immigrants, 22.6 percent came from white countries. 87.4 percent were from nonwhite countries. Taking the year 1979 as an example of recent legal immigration trends, the U.S. Immigration and Naturalization Service recorded 460,300 immigrants, of which 19.5 percent were from white countries, and 80.5 percent were from nonwhite countries. These figures are for legal and recorded immigrants. If, for that year, we estimate that illegal and unrecorded Mexican immigrants at only 2.5 million and the Asian and Pacific Island illegal and unrecorded immigrants at 0.5 million, that would mean that for the year 1979, 2.5 percent of the immigrants into America were white. Each year since 1979, America has seen a dramatic increase of nonwhite immigration, with 1985 estimated to have the highest number of nonwhite immigrants enter the United States of any prior year. This trend is not seen to be changing in the near future.

With an estimated 4 million illegal Mexican immigrants in 1983 alone, and a birth rate for Hispanics in America at 102 per 1000, compared with 71 per 1000 for whites,[23] the Latinization of the United States is particularly salient. The Population Reference Bureau, an independent Washington-based research group, estimated that Hispanics in America would increase to almost 50 million by 1990.[24]

As a result of current U.S. immigration policies, illegal immigration trends, high fertility rates of nonwhites, including Hispanics, low fertility rates of whites, and the growing occurrence of interracial marriage, unless measures are taken forthwith, in less than two decades, America will be more than 50 percent nonwhite, and in two more decades, white America will be virtually swept away.

## 3. Standards of Conduct Concerning the Family

### (a) Living Patterns

Just as the statistics and facts relating to race and demographics are often inaccurate and incomplete, so are the ones concerning living patterns in the United States. The actual condition of our society that each of us can observe firsthand often belies the statistics and reports compiled by the experts. There exists an inherent deficiency in statistics and surveys compiled from information gathered from the public in that individuals often misrepresent or color the truth for a variety of reasons ranging from ignorance to embarrassment to malicious design. In particular, personal situations that may reflect adversely on the individual are subject to an inordinate amount of misrepresentation. For example, during the 1930s, almost all states had a query concerning the legitimacy or illegitimacy of live births on their birth certificates.[25] This query produced statistics on which we estimated the illegitimate births of the nation. However, no adjustments were made for misstatements of legitimacy status on the birth record or for failure to register illegitimate births.[26] In all likelihood, many unwed mothers indicated that their children were legitimately born because of shame or fear of future ill-effects on their infants. Further, many unwed mothers never recorded the births at all. We cannot learn the true situation but we can conclude with certainty that a larger percentage of unwed mothers failed to record the birth of their children than did married mothers. This fact alone would skew the statistics away from reality. Accordingly, unless adjustment is made, it is likely that any statistics from the 1930s, or any other era as well, compiled to determine the ratio of illegitimate children to legitimate will underestimate the number of illegitimate births. There exists, however, no fault-free method of making such adjustments.

The entire field of statistics and information compilation suffers from the defects alluded to above. Often, an individual can obtain a better sense of the living patterns and social climate of his community through a subconscious survey of his own experiences than from a book of statistics and armful of surveys and facts compiled by even the most dedicated of statisticians. An individual citizen may take a mental survey of his community and be justified if his conclusions are in contradiction to surveys compiled by specialists. Nevertheless, in spite of the deficiencies inherent to statistics, we cannot ignore them and rely solely on our presumptions. In order to present an accurate portrait of the living patterns of our nation, we must gather together the available facts, statistics, and surveys, and then interpret them, if possible, in an enlightened manner. If the accuracy of such facts, statistics, and surveys is dubious, then they must be discredited. The real difficulty in using statistical information is in discerning truth from fiction. Common sense, in addition to mere numbers, must always be employed as a means of adjusting data for error. With all this in mind, let us now review the available statistics and other data which will give us an idea of the living patterns in America of today and yesterday.

According to the Bureau of the Census, in 1982, the traditional, or ideal, family with a male head of the household and the wife present comprised only 57.7 percent of the total households in America with the remaining 42.3 percent of the households consisting of single-parent families, divorced and widowed people, and those who have never married.[27] This 57.7 percent figure which is used to indicate the ratio of traditional families must be further adjusted downward because 4 percent of that total (3 percent of all households) are comprised of unmarried persons of the oppostie sex sharing living quarters. According to the Bureau of Census, there are 3.8 million persons cohabitating out of wedlock. This represents a fourfold increase over the 1970 census.[28] Included in the statistics for the "traditional family" are remarried divorcees. Thus, according to the census statistics, a family will still fall into the "traditional family" category even though its members may include an ex-husband, an ex-wife, stepchildren, stepparents, etc. Such a situation is hardly traditional or ideal.

In 1940, there were 34,949,000 households in the United States. 31,491,000 were families and 3,458,000 were individuals. 26,971,000 households had a husband and a wife present. This means that in 1940, households with both the husband and wife present comprised 77 percent of the total. Considering families only, excluding singles, 85 percent had the husband and wife present.[29] This compares with the 1982 figure of 57.7 quoted above. Further, in 1950, there were 43,554,000 households with 38,838,000 families and 4,716,000 individuals. Households with a husband and wife present comprised 34,440,000. In 1950, 79 percent of all households consisted of husband and wife and 89 percent of all families had a husband and wife present.[30]

The divorce rate in America doubled between 1965 and 1976[31] and is still accelerating. According to statistics derived from the Bureau of the Census, there are currently 10 divorcees for every 1000 married people and that in

1983, the number of married couples with children actually declined from 1970.[32] (It should be noted that the divorce column includes only those who are currently divorced and have not remarried and the married column includes divorcees who have remarried.) The statistics and trends show that one out of every two marriages will end in divorce.[33] Statistics from an Identity Research Institute study lead some researchers to conclude that "in some West Coast highly-populated counties the *real* divorce rate is running at 70 per cent, and in fact 75 per cent of marriages are 'bust.'"[34] Remarriage often occurs between two divorcees or between a divorcee and someone who was never married, with these remarriages often ending in divorce as well. These statistics indicate that today there is hardly a family which has not been affected by divorce either directly or indirectly. Even though a particular marriage may remain intact it is almost certain that either the couple's parents, children, or children's spouses have suffered or will suffer through a divorce. This would indicate that the traditional American family has almost disappeared.

### (b) Sexual Relations Outside of Marriage

In the 1940s and 1950s, the average high school student was chaste; in the 1980s, "teenage sex is a fact of life."[35] Between 1970 and 1982, the number of unwed mothers rose by 367 percent.[36] According to the National Center for Health Statistics, 48.3 percent of the births to teenage mothers were illegitimate. In 1980 there were 562,330 births to teenage mothers; of that figure, 271,801 were born out of wedlock.[37]

Surveys conducted at the University of California at Davis revealed that premaritial intercourse among students at that institution rose sharply in recent years to 62 percent by 1977 and 64 percent in 1981.[38] *Time* magazine states that America's promiscuity level has reached a ceiling with about 50 percent to 60 percent of college women active sexually.[39]

In 1984, the Census Bureau reported that the number of unmarried couples living together has more than tripled since 1970.[40] In the 1960s, the number of unmarried couples living together increased eightfold.[41] In 1983, about one in 25 couples living together was not married.[42]

Some 10 million to 20 million Americans have genital herpes with 200,000 to 500,000 new cases appearing each year.[43] In 1958, a little more than 200,000 cases of gonorrhea were reported. In 1976, that figure rose to roughly one million,[44] and in 1984 to 2 million.[45] Historically, before the current rage of genital herpes, and other recent venereal disease epidemics, syphilis ranked as the third most reported communicable disease in the United States, exceeded only by gonorrhea and chicken pox. Between 85,000 and 90,000 cases have been reported in recent years.[46] The sexually transmitted disease, chlamydia trachomatis, a burning infection of the reproductive and urinary system, affects an estimated 3 to 10 million people annually.[47] Nongonococcal sexually transmitted infections of the genito-urinary tract affect 2.5 million people annually. Crab lice, veneral warts and other bacterial, fungal or virus infections of the genitals, eyes, throat and blood affect many millions of individuals as well.[48] It is estimated that approximately 300,000 Americans are currently carriers of the deadly Acquired Immunity Deficiency Syndrome (AIDS), a disease primarily afflicting homosexuals.[49]

The above statistics demonstrate that American sexual ethics are totally opposite that of earlier eras. One need not look to Puritan America to find this contrast. In the 1940s and 1950s, America was disciplined in its sexual activity but not particularly extreme.

### (c) Abortion

Prior to 1967, a pregnant woman could not legally obtain an abortion in the United States except when it was necessary to save her life or preserve her health.[50] From 1967 until the U.S. Supreme Court's definitive ruling in 1972, several states made a number of changes liberalizing the restrictions against abortion. In 1972, the U.S. Supreme Court, in *Roe vs. Wade*[51] created a right to privacy which encompasses a woman's decision whether or not to abort her child, and that therefore (i) no state may interfere with or regulate her decision to abort in the first trimester of pregnancy, and (ii) no state may regulate the abortion during the second trimester of pregnancy except to the extent that the regulation is limited to the preservation of maternal health.

In 1973, 615,831 recorded abortions were performed. In 1976, 988,267 abortions were performed; in 1979, 1,251,921 abortions were performed.[52] In 1982, according to a recent survey funded by the Planned Parenthood Federation, 1,573,900 abortions were performed in the United States.[53] In Washington D.C., in 1975, there were 2.3 abortions for every live birth.[54]

### (d) Homosexuality

A generation ago, there were few open homosexuals; today, there are an estimated 16 million adults that society recognizes as homosexuals.[55] In 1973, the authors of *American Jurisprudence* presumed that the maximum penalty that could be imposed by the court for engaging in a homosexual act was capital punishment, inasmuch as under the common law, sodomy was a felony punishable by death.[56] In the 1950s and 1960s, homosexuals were routinely jailed for their acts.[57] In the 1980s, a *Los Angeles Times* poll found that 44 percent of the people did not oppose the homosexual lifestyle and 47 percent of the people said that the homosexality of a candidate for local office would not influence their vote.[58] "Homosexual characters and plot lines are becoming acceptable to TV network programmers."[59] San Francisco has avowed homosexuals as Municipal Judges[60] and allows homosexuals to adopt children.[61]

In 1980, the Pennsylvania Court held that a "voluntary deviate sexual intercourse statute which defined sexual intercourse as sexual intercourse per os (mouth) and per anus between human beings who are not husband and wife, and any form of sexual intercourse with animals, had only one possible purpose; regulation of private conduct of consenting adults." The court found that such purpose exceeded valid bounds of police power and infringed the right to equal protection.[62]

Recent Court decisions have held that it constitutes a violation of the constitutional guaranty of due process to dismiss a person from federal employment simply because of his homosexuality, without a showing of a rational connection between the employee's behavior and the efficiency of the government service.[63] The court said in *Society for Individual Rights, Inc. v. Hampton*[64] that although a homosexual's conduct may be deemed immoral by a majority of our society, this alone does not justify denying such a person government employment.

It has recently been held by our courts that a school board's policy of refusing to hire homosexuals as teachers violated fourteenth amendment guarantees of equal protection and due process.[65] The court in *Acanfora v. Board of Education,*[66] referring to the wide range of interests which courts had found to be protected by the fourteenth amendment as "essential to the orderly pursuit of happiness by free men" stated that the time had come for private, consenting, adult homosexuality to enter the sphere of constitutionally protectable interests.

In a divorce action between fundamentalist Christian, Betty Lou Batey, and her husband, Frank Batey, who turned homosexual, the court awarded the parents joint custody of their son. When Betty Lou took her son to Colorado, away from the father's homosexual influence, the San Diego Superior Court ordered her jailed. She subsequently faced charges of kidnapping.[67]

The courts have also held that a man "married" to a transsexual was lawfully married, had to pay alimony and had a duty to support "her" when he abandoned "her."[68]

## 4. Standards of Conduct Concerning the Community

### (a) Religion

In 1957, respondents to a Gallup Poll on the influence of religion in America felt overwhemingly that religion had an increasing influence on American life. Almost 70 percent felt that religious influence was increasing, while only 14 percent felt that it was losing influence.[69] By 1970, only 14 percent felt religious influence was increasing and 75 percent felt that it was decreasing.[70] According to a survey of the National Opinion Research Center in 1972, 35 percent of the American public attended church or other religious service at least once a week.[71] In 1977, that percentage dropped to 27.6 percent.[72] Prior to 1962, schools in many states had voluntary daily prayers and Bible readings. In 1962, the U.S. Supreme Court declared those acts to be unconstitutional.[73]

Religion has traditionally played a premiere role in the lives of the American people and the building of this nation. Indeed, America was colonized and founded expressly for religious reasons. The Mayflower Compact demonstrates the religious convictions of America's first settlers who had, in part, "undertaken for the Glory of God, and the Advancement of the Christian Faith a Voyage to plant the first colony in the northern part of Virginia."[74]

### (b) Crime

Throughout the late 1960s and into the early 1970s, the incidence of crime increased dramatically.[75] In 1957, there were 5 murders, 8 rapes (including statutory cases), 39 robberies, and 65 aggravated assaults reported for every 100,000 people.[76] By 1980, there were 10.2 murders, 36.4 rapes (excluding statutory cases), 243.5 robberies and 290.6 aggravated assaults reported for every 100,000 people.[77] These statistics are based upon reported incidents of crime. Unreported and undocumented incidents would push the rate much higher.

On a positive note, however, a 1984 Justice Department survey indicated a 2 percent decrease in the number of households victimized by crime in 1983 when compared with the previous year. In 1982, the percentage of American homes touched by crime was 29.3 percent. In 1983 it was 27 per cent.[78] Further, during this same period, violent crime fell by 10 percent and victimizations fell by 7 percent to 36.9 million.[79]

Steven Schlesinger, head of the Justice Department's Bureau for Justice Statistics, said the drop in victimization rates was due to several factors, including sentencing changes, shifts in population and "Neighborhood Watch" programs. He said, "The increasing willingness of judges to send convicted felons to prison, which is reflected in record-high incarceration rates, may act as a deterrent by the message it sends to potential criminals."[80]

### (c) Drug Abuse

Illicit drug use reached $50 billion annually by 1979.[81] Americans spend $25 billion a year on marijuana and $20 billion a year on cocaine.[82] New York City alone has 177,500 heroin addicts, nearly 1 person in 40,[83] and, as of late 1983, in the lower East side of New York City, there were at least 31 locations that openly sold heroin and 34 that sold cocaine.[84] A 1983-84 Gallup Organization on teenage drug abuse revealed the following:[85]

–12 percent of American teenagers admitted to "being into 'polydrugs' (combining alcohol with other drugs), a practice medical authorities describe as the most dangerous of all drug habits." This is one in eight teenagers;

–59 percent of American youth between the ages of 13 and 18 drink alcohol. Only 23 percent say they do not drink which is "the smallest figure ever recorded in these surveys;"

–7 percent between the ages of 16 and 18 use cocaine.

### (d) Entertainment

In areas of entertainment in recent years, our tastes have become lewd and less refined. In 1959, recordings by the Mormon Tabernacle Choir were favorite listening fare for millions of average Americans. "It was impossible to avoid hearing [the Choir] several times during a typical day of radio listening, as disc jockeys featured [them] in their top tune play lists."[86] They were among the most popular recording artists of the year and were grammy award winners. By contrast, in 1984, among the most popular recording artists was a group called "Culture Club," featuring a transvestite lead singer named "Boy George."[87]

Our movies and books typically contain great amounts of nudity and profanity and portray the lowest standard of morality, and our legal system condones this. An actor who refused to take off his clothes for a movie scene in a movie already under production received a Los Angeles Superior Court summons ordering him "to comply with all orders of the producer."[88] Our television shows, also containing profanity, involve protagonists who not only are bad role models, but who are often homosexuals, adulterers, and even perpetrators of incest.[89] Each of these forms of entertainment is considered to be mainstream and for the common man. Peep shows, sex acts performed live on stage, legalized prostitution and hardcore pornography are forms of entertainment that are not mainstream but are widely patronized.

In 1981, two of the top 15 magazines in number of issues sold were pornographic, namely *Playboy* and *Penthouse*.[90] The total monthly circulation of the most popular, over-the-counter pornographic magazines such as *Playboy, Penthouse, Hustler, Playgirl, Oui,* and *Cheri* totaled more than 13 million issues.[91] Smaller circulation, specialty, and underground pornography total many millions more. Americans spend approximately $7 billion per year on hardcore pornography. There are approximately 750 hardcore pornography motion picture houses in the United States, not including those showing pornographic homosexual movies.[92]

Thirty years ago, prior to *Playboy's* and others' challenge to our stance on pornography, there were no above-ground magazines that were explicit in their pandering to the sexual interests of the public.[93] Nor was there profanity or nudity in the movies, and television provided mainly uplifting entertainment. In the 1950s, the family in the "Donna Reed Show" prayed together.[94] In the 1980s, the families on "Dallas" and "Dynasty" commit every evil conceivable.[95]

### (e) Litigation

In 1982, more than 8 million civil actions were filed in the state and federal courts at a cost of about $2.2 billion to taxpayers to process them.[96] In 1983, more than 240,000 new civil actions were filed in federal courts, twice the number filed in 1975.[97] In California alone, 170,000 divorce cases are filed every year. (This represents about one-third of the civil case load.)[98] In recent years, the civil cases concerned every grievance and plaintiff imaginable, ranging from lawsuits brought by a child against Borden, Inc., for not giving her a prize in her Cracker Jack box[99] to a more than ten-year-long antitrust action brought by the U.S. Government against IBM, which produced more than 66 million pages of documents and cost IBM over $50 million in legal fees paid to its outside legal counsel.[100] In 1984, a nine-year-old boy who claimed in a suit that his mother and grandparents were negligent in watching over him as an infant when he severely burned his lips, was awarded $2 million against them. The parents' and grandparents' insurance company was ordered to pay the money to the boy.[101]

In one narrow and recently developed area, civil rights employment cases, 7,689 actions were filed in U.S. District Courts in 1982, a more than 750 percent increase over the 1972 figure.[102] As for criminal cases, 4,522 appeals were filed in the U.S. Courts of Appeals in 1982, concerning such crimes as homicide, robbery, drug abuse and illegal immigration. In 1982, federal and state prisoners filed a total of 29,303 petitions for motions to vacate sentence, habeas corpus, civil rights, mandamus, etc. compared with just over 2,000 in 1960.[103]

There are more than 620,000 practicing lawyers in the United States with 35,000 law students graduating each year from law schools. That makes one lawyer for every 375 Americans. In the mid-1990s, it is projected that there will be one attorney for every 260 people. In 1960, there were only 250,000 attorneys or one for every 632 people.[104] In 1980, the legal profession accounted for about 1.4 percent of the nation's gross national product.[105]

## 5. Standards of Conduct Concerning Industry

### (a) Poverty

In 1980, roughly one out of seven Americans was living below the official poverty level.[106] In 1982, the total poor numbered more than 34 million or 15 percent of the population.[107] In 1982, for Hispanics, the percentage of poor was 29.9 percent and for blacks, 35.6 percent.[108] According to the House of Representatives' Select Committee on Children, Youth and Family, one out of five children and one out of two black children in America now live in poverty-stricken families. Between 1980 and 1982, the number of poor children increased by 2 million.[109]

Where in 1982, 15 percent of the population lived below the poverty level, in 1973, the poor constituted only 11.1 percent.[110] The 34 million poor remain below the poverty level despite the fact that in 1980, a typical year, the federal government alone (not including state and local governments) expended $307 billion for social programs.[111] In 1985, the estimated outlays will be $459 billion.[112] In 1960, social spending represented 5 percent of the nation's gross national product; in 1984, it was 11.6 percent.[113]

The 1982 overall poverty rate of 15 percent is the highest rate since 1965, when the rate was 17.3 percent.[114] The following year the Bureau of the Census revised their methodology which significantly reduced the poverty rate.[115] The 1982 poverty rate for whites was 12 percent, compared with 8.4 percent in 1973.[116] The 1982 poverty rate for blacks of 35.6 percent is the highest rate since 1967 when the rate was 39.3 [117] The 29.9 percent poverty rate for Hispanics is the highest since the figures were compiled on them. In spite of the billions of dollars spent each year by various government agencies for welfare-related programs, the number of poor has been increasing. In particular it should be noted that a disproportionately larger share of these government funds go to support the swelling number of Hispanic, Negro and other minorities. These government funds are generated by taxes levied on the American people. Due to the graduated income tax structure, higher income earners have their income taxed at a greater percentage than the lower income earners who, at the very bottom, pay no taxes at all. Whites are disproportionately higher income earners than minorities but have only 12 percent of their numbers at the poverty level or below who would receive government assistance.

### (b) Education

According to our almanacs, we still claim to have a 99 percent literacy rate as we had in past eras.[118] Further, larger percentages of high school and college graduates pass through our institutions of education, and our students attend school for many more years than their counterparts in previous generations. Yet, in spite of this, the educational level of our youth is deteriorating dramatically and they learn much less today even though they live in a more complex world.

In the spring of 1983, the National Commission on Excellence in Education charged that "a rising tide of mediocrity [in the schools] threatens our very future as a nation."[119] The report, *A Nation at Risk*, asserts that if an enemy nation had forced the U.S. to accept today's low educational standards, "we might well have viewed it as an act of war. As it stands, we have allowed this to happen to ourselves."[120] Similarly, the Carnegie Foundation report argues that "the teaching profession is in a crisis in this country," and the National Task Force on Education for Economic Growth claims that "a real emergency is upon us," with more than 26 million Americans who are functionally illiterate.[121]

In 1963, the average SAT scores in America for both male and female seniors who were college-bound was 478 verbal and 502 math. In 1973, the average SAT scores for this same group were 445 verbal and 481 math. In 1977, scores were 429 verbal and 470 math. And in 1981, they were 424 verbal and 466 math.[122] This shows a steady decline since the early 1960s in the true educational level of our children.

According to *A Nation at Risk*, performance by high school students on standardized tests is worse today than at any time since 1957.[123] It is estimated that on any one day in New York City, 50 percent of the students are absent from school.[124] By contrast, daily attendance at Japan's schools averages 98 percent.[125] About 13 percent of all 17-year olds in the United States are "functionally illiterate." They cannot read basic material or follow a set of simple directions.[126]

### (c) Industry and Technology

In 1960, America's economy made up 33.7 percent of the world's economy; in 1980, that margin shrunk to 21.5 percent.[127] Japan more than tripled its share of the world economy during the same period. Its economy rose from 2.9 percent to 9.0 percent.[128] From 1870 to 1970, the United States almost always exported more than it imported. In the 1970s, this trend began to change. Currently, the U.S. foreign trade deficit "could balloon to about $140 billion for 1985."[129]

Observers note that: Regarding America's world economic competitiveness, "America and the world have entered a zone of disorder and danger seldom, if ever, equalled in human experience;"[130] and that, "America has got to increase productivity or it will be on the road to oblivion. This is a strange statement, I know, but believe me it is true. Japan's productivity shot up 80 percent over the last decade while ours increased by only 15 percent."[131]

In 1950, the world production of motor vehicles was 10,577,813 of which the United States manufactured 8,005,859 or 75.7 percent of the total.[132] Japan manufactured 31,597 or 0.3 percent.[133] Today, America produces millions fewer motor vehicles than it did in 1950. In 1981, the world production of motor vehicles more than tripled to 37,550,845 while the United States production declined to 7,942,916 or 21.2 percent of the total world production.[134] Japan's share rose to 11,179,962 or 30 percent.[135] In 1950, world pig iron production (including ferroalloys) totalled 146,381,747 tons.[136] The United States production was 65,439,769 tons, or 41 percent of the world total.[137] In 1965, world production was 360,544,000 tons and U.S. production was 88,858,672 tons, or 24.6 percent of the world total. In 1982, the preliminary world total of pig iron production was 550,815,000 tons compared with the United States preliminary total production of 43,136,000 tons or 7.8 percent of the world total.[138]

In 1978, America's merchant fleet with 12 million tons sailing under its flag, is dwarfed by Japan's 29 million gross tons, Great Britian's 33 million, Norway's 28 million, and Greece's 23 million.[139] Rep. Paul S. Trible Jr. (R.,Va.) pointed out in the House that: "The U.S. merchant marine, being noncompetitive in costs of construction and operation, continues to decline. American flag shipping, by total volume, is carrying less than 6 percent of all U.S. foreign trade and commerce."[140] In 1975, U.S. flag carriers transported 5.1 percent of all U.S. cargo.[141] American tankers took part in the movement of 4.6 percent of the oil imported and exported.[142] Carriage of bulk commodities by U.S. flag ships amounted to 1.4 percent.[143]

U.S. shipyards are unable to compete with foreign shipbuilders who offer to build merchant vessels at prices 60 percent lower than it will cost in the United States.[144] With rare exceptions, U.S. shipbuilders must rely on military and domestic shipping procurement protected under federal law. During 1983, shipbuilding declined by 14 percent.[145] The current orderbook for commercial vessel production is at a pre-World War II level. Only 12 deep-draft commercial vessels, 1,000 gross tons and over, are projected to be under construction or on order as of January 1, 1984.[146] In contrast, world orderbook of vessels of 2,000 dead weight tons or more was 1,442.[147]

In 1977, the United States machine tool industry imports accounted for only 15.6 percent of the market.[148] In 1983, foreign manufacturers, primarily Japanese, have taken 47 percent of the market.[149]

Regarding consumer electronics, in 1960, the United States manufactured 17.2 million radio sets.[150] Today, the only radios manufactured in the United States are some car stereos.[151] In 1960, the United States manufactured 5.7 million televisions,[152] or almost 30 percent of the world total. By 1976, it manufactured 6 million sets,[153] or only about 15 percent of the world's total. In 1984, the U.S. manufactured even a smaller percentage. During the past 25 years the domestic consumer electronics industry has shifted from being a principal supplier of traditional radio and television receivers and related products to being the minority supplier. Imports account for an estimated 56 percent of sales in the domestic market.[154]

U.S. manufacturers no longer produce monochrome television receivers, domestic demand is met by imports from the Far East.[155] Portable and table radios and audio tape recorders are not produced in the U.S. Production has shifted to the Far East.[156] The U.S. does not produce consumer-type video cassette recorders.[157] Few U.S. firms manufacture dot-matrix impact printers.[158] The U.S. manufactures virtually no 35mm cameras.[159] Only one U.S.-owned company manufacturers motorcycles and it has been losing money yearly.[160]

The rate of savings in the U.S. is the lowest of any developed country. Personal savings rate in Japan is 19 percent; in France, 16 percent; in West Germany, 14 percent; in Britain, 14 percent and in the U.S. less than 5 per cent.[161] When business needs more capital than ever, we are selling more stock than we are buying. In 1970, there were 31 million individual investors. Today, there are only 24 million.[162]

### (d) Public Works

"America's infrastructure—the vast, vital network of roads, bridges, sewers, rails and mass-transit systems—is heading toward collapse. The decay is most acute in older industrial cities, but clogged highways and strained water systems also threaten to strangle booming Sun Belt towns . . . "[163]

Half of Conrail's rails and roadbeds are seriously decayed.[164] One-half of all American communities cannot expand because their water-treatment systems are at or near capacity.[165] One of every five bridges in the U.S. are so dangerously deficient they are either restricted or closed.[166] Transportation Secretary Drew Lewis says we are "living on our laurels of the 1950s and 1960s."[167] In 1977, the Army Corp of Engineers inspected nearly 9,000 dams out of the nation's total of 68,000, and found roughly one-third to be unsafe, with 130 in danger of imminent collapse.[168]

## 6. In Conclusion

The above facts unequivocally indicate that America is:

1. becoming a nonwhite nation;
2. allowing its family structure to dissolve;
3. engaging in rampant sexual promiscuity directly resulting in:
   a) an elimination of chastity;
   b) widespread abortion;
   c) widespread and open homosexuality; and
   d) rampant heterosexual and homosexual venereal disease;
4. losing its faith in God and its Christian ethics;
5. beset with uncontrollable crime;
6. beset with widespread drug abuse;
7. promoting decadence through its forms of entertainment;
8. contentious and litigious;
9. allowing the numbers of poor to swell enormously;
10. losing its national literacy;
11. losing its technological edge; and
12. allowing its public works to decay.

# II.  DECLINE AND RUIN

## 1. Definition

Based upon the facts and statistics set forth in Chapter I and upon the changes occurring in our society, as viewed in the context of world history and development, it is sadly apparent that in recent years America has been declining and, in fact, is on the brink of collapse and ruin. Unless drastic measures are taken forthwith, the country established by our forefathers "to secure the blessings of liberty to...our posterity"[169] will cease to exist.

It is not a far-reaching assertion to claim that America is on the brink of collapse and ruin. The statistics and facts of the previous chapter demonstrate that America has experienced rapid change, and that much of this change is undeniably for the worse. Any nation which experiences a diminishing technological edge, declining educational level, a growing underclass of hardcore poor, free use of narcotics and hallucinogens, widespread divorce, rampant immorality, abortion rates that at times exceed birth rates, uncontrollable crime, open and condoned homosexuality, and drastic changes in racial composition from a white society to a nonwhite society is indeed heading for a fall.

The terms "ruin" and "fall" imply a state of decay, degeneration and collapse, especially through natural processes.[170] The terms can connote, at the one extreme, destruction and even annihilation, and at the other, a mere breakdown.[171] To further define the terms "ruin" or "collapse" and our perception of them, I would like to point to the destruction of Pompeii and the Tasmanian aboriginies as examples. Ruin might apply to these two societies, but oblivion would be a more apt term. Ancient Rome became a ruined empire as did Greece, but this does not mean that all Romans or Greeks were destroyed as the Pompeians and Tasmanian aboriginies were, nor does it mean that the cities ceased to function or have laws to govern their people or that the people ceased to live under them. What occurred in ancient Greece and Rome was a ruin or collapse. This is the meaning that this text employs in its evaluation of America's situation, not total oblivion without any vestiges of our civilization remaining, but a destruction in the form of a fall with certain aspects of America remaining, but its structure and composition drastically altered.

Depending upon one's frame of reference, what one person perceives as ruin may, to another person, appear to be only an injury and to a third person even a revival. For example, in the mind of one person, a wilderness fire may constitute the destruction of a forest. To a second person, it may be perceived only as an injury to the forest. And to a third person, it may be perceived as a revival, by clearing the foliage to allow new growth. All three theories may have merit, and even though the third person's conclusion is radically opposed to the opinions of the first two, the third person should certainly be allowed by the other two to possess his opinion. However, this does not entitle the third person to further his beliefs by setting forest fires or by hindering the first two from extinguishing them. These principles on ruin are applicable to societies as well as forests except that with our society, there seem to be more pyromaniacs.

Individuals who view racial, linguistic and cultural diversification, homosexuality, pornography and unrestricted sexual license as refreshing changes from an old, staid system may be permitted to harbor those views, but when they are allowed to take action to further those views, and particularly, when they constitute a large portion of society, the rest of the denizens of the woods must step forward to counter such views or risk losing their whole forest to the flames.

## 2. Primary Areas of Ruin: Standards of Conduct and Racial Identity

The decline and ruin of America, as demonstrated by the facts and statistics in Chapter I, can be divided into two primary areas: standards of conduct and identity. Standards of conduct encompasses the various topics categorized in Chapter I under "Family," "Community," and "Industry." Identity includes our racial and cultural heritage. These two areas are interrelated, each contributing to decline in the other. For example, our changing racial composition has, in part, resulted in increased illiteracy rates,[172] poverty rates,[173] crime rates,[174] infant mortality rates,[175] physical and mental defects[176] and decreased production levels.[177] By contrast, a singular heritage and racial makeup of a community and reverence therefor encourages uniformity in moral and ethical principles and enables the community to more effectively police itself. A close-knit, uniform society can better encourage high morals and standards of conduct than can a diverse one.

Further, our changing standards of conduct concerning children and the traditional family, sexual relations and religious beliefs result in an acceleration in the change of America's racial composition. As a consequence of these changing concepts, white Americans bear fewer children than minorities[178] and incidents of miscegenation increase.[179]

There are times when issues regarding standards of conduct and identity appear to be interrelated and cross over from one area to another when in reality a distinct separation could be maintained. For example, advocates of racial intergration (an issue concerning identity) often try to apply principles of morality (a type of standard of conduct) to support their cause and to suppress opposition thereto. It is often said in our society that race and integration of the races is a moral issue and advocation of an all-white (or all-black) society is morally wrong[180] when, in reality, principles of morality might not apply.

People should have the right to maintain a community and a country for themselves and their posterity, without feeling morally compelled to integrate that community or country with different peoples. And where a considerable amount of integration has occurred in a society, the people should still have the right to maintain or return to a society comprised only of its own people. The actions of such a society should not necessarily be characterized as moral or immoral. The problems a society confronts in this regard concern the issues of identity, heritage and race and not necessarily morality. The only time the issue of morality should be applicable to this problem would be in the action the society institutes to secure the community for its own people. At the point the society decides to maintain a community or a country for its own people to the exclusion of other peoples who either temporarily or permanently reside within its borders, the issue of morality should come into play only in determining the proper scope and method employed by the one people to achieve this end. When the rights of two separate peoples conflict, it is not a moral issue that the rights of one people prevail, but the issue of morality might be considered to mitigate the actions taken.

The ruin of America has commenced already and without remedial action will be complete in this generation. As is apparent from the facts and statistics, America is crumbling on many fronts, but the most direct, the most irreversible, the most explosive force causing America's collapse concerns race. The American people are being replaced by other races who are now also considered to be Americans. Therein lies the ruin. When this transition is complete, Los Angeles, for example, will still exist as a city with the U.S. Constitution ostensibly governing its people, but it will not be America even if it retains that title, and the people will not be Americans: they will be a new people calling themselves Americans. The semantical application of the term "American" to the new inhabitants will not alter the reality of the situation which is that the American people will have been replaced by a different people as surely as if hostile forces armed with superior weapons invaded the nation, subjugated the inhabitants and gained possession through war.

The replacing of a white people for a nonwhite people, a Western European culture for a Latin and Oriental culture, and the English language for the Spanish language are obvious manifestations of the collapse and ruin to which I refer. In fact, the replacing of one people for another, is the direct tangible force of the ruin. This is the ruin that concerns our identity. However, there are also many less obvious but equally severe manifestations of ruin, which concern our standards of conduct, such as the collapse of our industry, our educational system, our values, and our family structure.

## 3. Action Must be Taken

To reverse America's decline and avert a ruin or collapse, we must recognize our situation and agree upon a course for change. Changes will need to be made in standards of conduct and identity. The barriers for change, that is, the impediments to our instituting measures to alter our present decline, are threefold. First, we must recognize our incorrect beliefs and attitudes concerning our standards of conduct and identity. We must also alter our end in life from an overemphasis on self-gratification and individual fulfillment, to one of securing a future for ourselves and our posterity. The actions of too many Americans reflect an attitude similar to the French aristocracy of the 1770s and Louis XV who, devoting himself to carnal pleasure, declared: *"Apres moi le deluge"* — "After me, the flood." And as it was with them so it may be with us.

This recognition of our incorrect beliefs and desire for change will be the most challenging barrier of all. We have developed elaborate rationalizations to justify our present bad acts and ignore the realities of our decline. Hence, we often no longer discern good from bad and progression from regression. When we confront the present collapse of our standards of conduct, many of us act like the criminal inventing excuses to justify his crime. And when we confront our present collapse of heritage and racial identity, many of us act like the insane, withdrawing into a make-believe world, finding solace for an uncomfortable existence through a framework of imaginary beliefs—imaginary beliefs that America can thrive as a multiracial nation, that race does not matter and that our country will still stand when we lose control of it. The most difficult task of all is convincing the criminal to abandon his excuses, or the mentally withdrawn to grasp reality. This is the first barrier for America in altering its destructive course of action.

Once recognition of our incorrect beliefs and attitudes as to standards of conduct and identity is made, the second step is for us to concur in the measures needed to alter our course. In such a fractionalized and so-called independently thinking society which exists today, this task will be difficult.

Finally, the American people must exert sufficient effort in sufficient numbers to effect the changes. Even though this last barrier requires the most physical action on the part of the American people, it will be the easiest to accomplish, for, just as we have done in past crises, once we recognize our condition and the regressive acts and attitudes that have caused it and concur in the remedial measures, our zeal and concern should foster sufficient motivation to effect the necessary changes.

There are many different types of people in America who face different barriers in recognizing our decline and in our taking affirmative remedial action. Some Americans will recognize and support, at least in spirit, action to both return our society to a higher standard of conduct and to preserve our racial identity and heritage. Others will only recognize and support action in either the area of standards of conduct or identity, but not both. They may either advocate a return to a racially united America, but not wish to exert the effort to raise America's standards of conduct or may advocate a higher standard of conduct and a racially mixed society. According to the latest trends, America is awakening to the need for higher standards of conduct,[181] and Americans are also beginning to desire to live with their own people again.[182] However, since the numbers of nonwhites are increasing so rapidly, the number of Americans desiring a mixed or colored America grows as well. Moreover, in spite of the advocacy of many for a mixed America, such a permanent arrangement is not possible. A racially mixed America is only a transition to a homogeneous society. As peoples integrate, they intermarry, and as they intermarry, they become one people again. The ultimate result of an integration of America is the coloring of its people and the loss of its European heritage.

The nonwhites in America will not advocate a return to a white America since this could mean involuntary displacement for them and they generally are in this country of their own choice and out of a desire to stay. Once the number of nonwhites and whites who incorrigibly desire to live in a mixed or colored America grows too large, change will no longer be possible and ultimate coloring of the people will result. This unchangeable situation will occur in our democracy when there are no longer enough white Americans to take action to secure their rights and heritage.

For this reason, the issue of identity may be more pressing than standards of conduct and action thereon must be taken more swiftly. Since it is human nature to be clannish, to identify with one's family, race and people and to desire to preserve one's self and one's posterity, it should be easier to convince Americans of the principles in support of their identity and heritage than to convince them to support a higher standard of conduct since man is by nature carnal and undisciplined.

In the next chapters our incorrect beliefs and bad influences as to our standards of conduct and identity will be examined, and discussion and necessary changes will be presented. The discussion may be controversial and deal with sensitive issues, but only by dealing with them directly will we be able to determine our own destiny. If we ignore the issues because they are sensitive, then our nation will be shaped by the trends rather than shaped by us.

# III. ANALYSIS OF PHILOSOPHIES WHICH FOSTER OUR DECLINE — PART ONE

## 1. Introduction

Through man's intelligence and ability to reason, he can manipulate and direct his course of action and his fate. Nevertheless, his reasoning can be a trap and his complexity can cause him to stumble. Man must be careful in his reasoning and use of intelligence because through them he creates an artificial and complex world that is an extension of the natural environment. Man must still confront nature and natural principles, but he must also grapple with his own man-made situations that can and do exceed the average individual's ability to control them. For example, a man may know how to engage a switch to fill his room with light. He may even understand how to wire his house to provide light in every room, but he may not understand the details of the generation of electricity or be able to confront and solve problems at the electrical source. Thus group effort is essential, and responsibilities are divided within a society according to need and skill. Man can devise complexities that individuals, groups and even whole societies are unable to cope with and solve. Literally speaking, man would never be so foolish to wind himself around a pole until he strangles to death as a tethered cow would do. Such an act of self-destruction, being apparent to an intelligent creature, would be avoided without second thought. Man would fall victim only to much more complex and less apparent traps. Nevertheless, the principle could be the same: he could be tethered to particular ideologies and rationalizations, and any attempt at progress while so tethered could result in only circular motion, causing him to wrap himself tighter and tighter around the anchor until he expires.

In recent years, much of America has tethered itself to a series of errant philosophies concerning its standards of conduct and racial identity, which has caused it to travel in circles toward ultimate strangulation.

On many issues, America has rationalized and compromised vital social principles, and every time a principle is compromised, society is adversely affected. When such a principle is violated by a sizeable portion of the population, the adverse impact thereof is magnified greatly. For example, if one family in a community is broken up through divorce, the impact on the community may not be great. But when half of all marriages or more in a community break up, the entire social structure is endangered. It is a simple premise that from a small amount of bad comes only a little harm and from a large amount of bad comes great harm.

Our acts of rationalization and compromise are dangerous on two counts: (1) it often becomes difficult to discern good from bad because rationalization is artfully invented and, (2) rationalization abets the commission of bad acts. When an individual is confronted with a situation that has two courses of action available, and there exists philosophical arguments supporting both courses, the individual will often be inclined to take the easier or more self-gratifying course of action. Even when the philosophical grounds for supporting the easier or baser course of action are weak, the easier or baser course of action has the advantage because of man's propensity to do what is easy or pleasurable. Rationalization can thereby provide an excuse to commit bad acts. Through complex forms of rationalization, we have established many incorrect philosophies and theories on which we base our actions. Since we are social animals governed by our principles, philosophies and theories, if these are faulty, then our society is imperiled.

Man is capable of using his intelligence to any end, even to conquer his urge to survive as a species. He can employ rationalization to overcome his sense of duty to his offspring. He is empowered with the ability to replace his instinct for survival of his species with a desire for self-gratification. For example, man is able to overcome the results of his sexual urges. He can obtain carnal pleasure without the responsibility of childbirth. When a child is conceived, man can choose to abort and find justification for such an act. Unlike in the animal world, which does not permit abandonment of responsibility to the young if the young are unable to fend for themselves, when a child is born, one or both parents are able to, and often do, abandon the child and reject their responsibility through divorce, desertion or otherwise. Further, unlike most animals, man is also capable of abusing its offspring. Such abuse can be physical, emotional or ideological. Physical abuse is generally considered the most outrageous and cruel, but ideological abuse, the most widespread, may be more destructive to society. A child who is taught by his parents, either through indoctrination or example, to gratify his base desires in pornography, homosexual or illicit heterosexual activities, drugs, and alcohol, who is encouraged to abandon the racial and cultural heritage of his homeland, and who is taught that morality and justice are relative and that intolerance of evil is evil itself, will grow up and live in his world unaware of the destruction that he is bringing upon himself. He will then die unaware of his errors. Other peoples who have not been so ideologically abused, will replace him in his own country.

## 2. Philosophies Regarding Standards of Conduct

### (a) In General: the Family, the Community and Standards of Conduct

The family and the community are the backbone of any society. The strength and character of a nation are formed and preserved therein. The family and community govern where laws cannot, and are such important factors in human life that every facet of existence revolves around them. They encompass all things, the past and the future, religion, morality, laws, customs, education, work, leisure, life and death. The family and the community are the units that, ultimately, must enforce all laws and further all customs, teach language, art and science. If the family and the community are defective, the nation is crippled. Although America should rightly concern itself with outside forces and should fear the spread of human bondage, the real and pervasive danger to our country is from within. America has been too mighty in terms of military strength to be invaded and conquered by brute force, but unstable families and our ineffective communities with decadent beliefs, misguided ideals and racial strife will cause our destruction more thoroughly than any army assembled in today's world.

It is a sad commentary on the American community when a campaign of the United States Army urges its personnel to be good citizens with the admonishment, "Dare to Be Different!"[183] What is the norm of the American community if the slogan "Dare to be Different" means: "Do not take drugs. Do not steal or violate the law. Work hard and respect authority?" This must mean that the norm of the American military community, a cross-section of our entire nation, is drug abuse, lawlessness, deceit, sloth and selfishness. This norm is all too consistent a pattern in today's society and consequently our communities and our families are becoming seriously flawed. These flaws leave us weak and subject to forces from without and within which are acting to our ruin. Below we will discuss some of the causes of our nation's pervasive defects and suggest corrective measures to avoid the ruinous results of our bad acts.

A most serious cause of the defects in our families, communities and industries is our standards of conduct, and a major aspect of our standards of conduct is our code of morals. Indeed, the term "standards of conduct" can be synonomous with the term "code of morals". In this text, however, the term "standards of conduct" is given a broader definition than the term "code of morals."

We often hear it said that morality is relative to society and subject to change with time and people. Moreover, many of today's thinkers aver that society cannot or should not legislate morality and that any attempt to do so will fail. They cite the ineffectiveness of the eighteenth amendment to the Constitution (prohibition)[184] to prove their point. When, in fact, the very purpose of laws is to legislate morality. The purpose of a code of morals is to govern the acts of society and enable it to distinguish between right and wrong conduct. Laws serve the very same purpose. The major distinction between these two methods of policing human conduct is that the code of morals is usually the basic, the most broad and informal measure of right and wrong conduct. Laws are specific in nature and address enumerated conduct. They are subject to interpretation, but interpretation which generally allows only two alternatives, guilt or absence of guilt. The code of morals is a system of comprehensive but uncodified principles which allow many shades of obedience or disregard whereby the individual is deemed to be moral or immoral. Since the code of morals is the basic measure of our conduct in society, when that code is rendered ineffective, or when certain major principles are eliminated, laws must be enacted to compensate and cover the areas that the code omits.

A code of morality is an anchor to society that keeps it stable, controllable and preserves it for use by future generations. To remove the moral code from society is to cut the moorings of a ship and let it drift away in a turbulent sea. Each new generaion would then have to construct a new ship, or society, until a preserving anchor is reattached. A society must be founded on moral principles or anarchy will prevail. As mentioned above, laws are inherently moral and some ideology or moral framework must be established to make the laws consistent with each other. Even with the existence of such moral framework, laws by themselves are not enough to govern the actions of the citizens. Laws may be established to cover major societal demands, such as statutes proscribing murder and theft. Moreover, laws may be established to deal with minor societal concerns such as laws on trespass or nuisance, but no society can enact laws to govern every action which should be governed to make the society a functional, much less a superior one. That task is reserved for the code of morals. Laws are not effective in forcing citizens to keep their idle promises, but societies can instill that principle into its citizens through its code of morals. Religious instruction handles that task effectively. Laws cannot effectively proscribe lying to one's wife or friend but religion and morality can.

America's efforts to guarantee maximum freedom of action to every individual has effectively emasculated that code and so we are no longer a moral people. It is an uncommon American who is honest in all his dealings. Thus our society suffers, not only because a dishonest and immoral society is an unpleasant and counterproductive place in which to live, but also because our reputation is lessened in the eyes of the world. Every bad act in a society harms that society and has an adverse impact on each individual therein. An individual living in society cannot but affect his society for good or for bad. If an individual lives a good, moral life, he not only makes his society stronger by virtue of his own membership therein, but he also influences his fellow citizens and helps elevate their standards. Conversely, an individual who engages in bad acts not only tears down society by his presence but by his acts he encourages others to do likewise, even when his bad acts are conducted wholly in private.

Our lack of high morals leaves holes in the structure of our society that we try to patch with awkward laws. When we sacrifice one major moral principle, we must enact many ridiculous little laws to cover the morass of problems that arise therefrom. For example, our society has ignored the principle of lifelong marital fidelity, with one result being a drastic increase in divorce. Divorce creates many additional problems, some of which our society tries to rectify through such legal concepts as "alimony",[185] "palimony",[186] "custody of the children",[187] "joint custody of the children",[188] and "joint custody of the pets."[189] The condition of today's society would be comical if it were not so destructive.

### (b) Standards of Conduct Concerning the Family

A loving home with honorable parents will do more to build a strong, harmonious, successful nation than any other factor conceivable. As is demonstrated by the facts and statistics set forth in Chapter I, the American family is no longer strong and stable. In our quest for more freedom, we are allowing this most important unit to dissolve. As stated above, one in two marriages today ends in divorce. Children are no longer being reared by both their parents but often only by their mothers. Our laws and our mores are now constructed in such a way that we no longer require our citizens to create a solid family unit. Casual sexual relations are not only legally permissible but are accepted in society. Few plots of the modern novel or movie are drafted without some casual sex woven into them. Thus the natural sexual urges are no longer a bond to bind a man and a woman together into a lifetime union. Men can find gratification on every corner and women have deceived themselves into believing that this is a right and a freedom they want to enjoy themselves. The vows of marriage are no longer a requirement for couples to live together. Couples mate and separate then regroup with other partners in such a casual, uncommitted manner that an observer would think we were fish of the sea. Animals generally have more commitment in a single relationship than Americans do. When a marriage ceremony is finally performed, it generally has no more social or legal power to bind than the parties themselves wish it to have. They may divorce, separate and copulate with others at will without fear of social consternation or punishment at law.

We will now examine some of our modern philosophies and beliefs that have contributed to this breakdown of the family unit.

### (i) Divorce

For much of our nation's history, divorce was a rare or unheard-of occurrence. Until recently, American courts and legislatures looked with extreme disfavor on the dissolution of marriage. Antebellum South Carolina, for example, had never granted a divorce: "The policy of this State has ever been against divorce. It is one of her boasts that no divorce has ever been granted in South Carolina."[190] The antebellum North Carolina court observed the following about divorce:[191] "We reconcile ourselves to what is inevitable. Experience finds pain more tolerable than it was expected to be; and habit makes even fetters light. Exertion, when known to be useless, is unassayed; though the struggle might be violent, if by possibility it could be successful. A married couple thus restrained may become, if not devoted in their affections, at least discreet partners, striving together for the common good."

Under common law, there was no absolute divorce decree.[192] Marriage, being one of the seven sacraments of the church, was absolutely insoluble if validly contracted.[193] Gradually, through America's evolutionary process toward unrestrained activity, our society came to accept the "fault" system of divorce. Typical divorce legislation up to the 1960s permitted divorce only where one party had been guilty of some serious violation of the marital contract, such as adultery, and the other party had been innocent of wrongdoing.[194]

In spite of these laws, most divorces were granted in noncontested default cases where the litigants were willing to enter into collusive litigation or commit perjury in order to effect the dissolution of their marriage.[195] This common and notorious practice inevitably had the effect of degrading the administration of justice and lowering the reputation of the bench and bar in the public esteem.[196]

Judges, lawyers, and legal scholars began advocating the nation to permit quick and easy divorces. Their rationale ranged from desire to conform the laws with the practice of society, to a baser desire of eradicating the restrictive barriers and mores of society and bring on "the sexual revolution." As early as the 1950s, judges such as Justice Samuel H. Silbert of Cuyahogan County, Illinois, Common Pleas Court, argued that the nation should not set up artificial barriers to divorce and such barriers sharply diminish the chances for a happy marriage.[197] Judge Silbert averred that some of these barriers were "children, religion, economic security, and, lastly, fear of what the neighbors might say."[198] Other legal theorists argued that divorce should have "equal dignity" with marriage and should be easily granted to enable the parties to "remember the beautiful experiences of their marriage."[199] Eventually, through change in the law or by custom of the jurisdiction, most states came to grant no-fault divorces and made marital separation easier than cashing a check at a strange bank.

It is into this slapdash union that today's baby, America's posterity, is born. It is to these sometimes irresponsible, uncommitted, free-spirited and unrestrained parents that the infant is charged. Proper rearing of a child is such a cornerstone to any society that laws and customs should be structured in a manner to promote that endeavor rather than allow the parents to escape responsibility in the name of freedom. State legislatures might want to reevaluate the benefit of no-fault divorce statutes on the public well-being. States might still recognize the harm in denying divorce in certain instances, yet see the value in making a divorce more difficult to obtain. Such would be an example of the application of W. E. Gladstone's observation: "It is the duty of the government to make it easy for the people to do right and difficult for the people to do wrong."[200]

A high divorce rate in a community is but one manifestation of the defects found in the family unit there. If measures are not taken to correct its other defects pertaining to the family at the same time as measures are taken to lower the divorce rate, then indeed, much harm may result from a denial of divorce. Restricting divorce can be one method in an overall program adopted by states to strengthen the family unit.

### (ii) Sexual Ethics

The sexual behavior and attitudes of a society are fundamental to its standards of conduct and code of morals. Indeed, the word "morality" is sometimes employed to mean specifically virtue in sexual conduct. Although, in general, it means "the character of being in accord with the principles or standards of right conduct."[201] Maybe, because temptation for abuse of our sexual ethics is so strong and the direct and indirect consequences of such abuse are so severe, no imperfect society can keep it in its proper perspective.

Some of the direct consequences of an abuse of our sexual ethics are, of course, illegitimate children, curable and incurable veneral disease, physical and mental damage to both juveniles and adults, and abortion. Some of the indirect consequences of widespread abuses are a disintegration of our family units, breakdown of discipline, work ethic and other aspects of our standards of conduct, and a disruption of the racial balance of the nation, which will result in the ultimate replacement of our dissipated and nonprocreating race with fecund ones. Indeed, an abuse of our sexual ethics may very well be the most fundamental flaw in our nation and might be the ultimate underlying cause of our decline and ruin. America might be proving, firsthand, that there was order and reason in our predecessor societies for the adoption and maintenance of a rigid code of sexual ethics.

In Chapter I, we examined some of the direct and indirect consequences of abuse of our sexual urges. At this point we shall examine the rationale and arguments employed by the advocates of relaxed moral standards, discuss the weaknesses therein and advocate a return to our traditional standards.

The sexual revolution had a history of evolution prior to its explosion in the 1960s. In the 1920s, works like *Ulysses* and *Lady Chatterly's Lover* were written in a manner that was viewed as tending to corrupt the morals of the era. These works were banned.[202] A French play, Edouard Bourdet's *The Captive*, mild by today's standards, about lesbianism was opened in New York but was closed by police.[203] In the 1940s and 1950s, writers, generally seeking acclaim through innovation and scandal rather than improvement of their art or of society, kept treading on conventional standards and wrote racier and racier passages. Courts in many jurisdictions banned such works while others did not.[204] The bannings added publicity and notoriety to the authors and their works so that a considerable number of persons from an otherwise uninformed public purchased the volumes and made flouting conventional standards profitable.

The 1940s cheesecake pinups such as those of Betty Grable, which showed bare legs and little else, gave way to partial and full nudity in such magazines as *Playboy* and *Confidential*. At that point, the sexual evolution stopped and the sexual revolution began. A clear indication of the rapid change in sexual ethics is the Ralph Ginzburg pornography case. He was convicted of distributing obscene material, and while his conviction was still being appealed (and ultimately upheld) by the U.S. Supreme Court, the New York Times reported that "a virtual revolution in sex and the arts has come about", making Ginzburg's obscene publication "look tame to many observers."[205]

The above examples detail the sexual revolution from the aspect of pornography and the first amendment concepts of freedom of speech. The other sex-related matters evolved in the same manner. The "free love" movement on the college campuses during the turbulent 1960s spread to middle-class America, the result being that where chastity and virginity had been the desired standard, it became something to be ashamed of and abandoned even at an early age. A similar but more precipitous pattern developed concerning abortion. In the late 1960s, New York changed its laws to permit a doctor to perform an abortion up to the sixth month of pregnancy.[205] Court rulings in Washington, D.C., and other jurisdictions against existing abortion laws had the same effect. Finally, in 1973, in *Roe v. Wade*,[206] the U.S. Supreme Court ruled anti-abortion laws to be unconstitutional.

The homosexual revolution, whose object is more deviant than other sexual practices and held in higher contempt by more people than is unchastity or pornography, began later and is still in the developing stages. As a result of the sexual revolution, America's morals sank to their lowest levels ever in her short history. Some of the more egregious examples of decadent philosophies will be easily rejected by the reader. Their destructive natures and baseless support will offer little reason for even the most "liberated" of readers to support them. These philosophies however, are proposed by a considerable number of "scholars" and "leaders of their field," and are supported by a sometimes large number of educated deviants. The fallacy and destructiveness of many of the less egregious examples of philosophies that abuse our sexual ethics are harder to discern. Yet proper discernment and rejection of these philosophies is just as necessary for the well-being of our society as the rejection of the egregious examples.

Below, without comment, are selected examples of the destructive philosophies of advocates of the "new morality." Some of these statements already show that they come from a different, less experienced and less jaded era. The statements are therefore often outdated. However, even if the statements appear outdated, their influence is still so strong that our society continues to struggle with their effects.

## 1. Incest

> [Rene] Guyon suggests that if we could look dispassionately and rationally at the principle of sexual pleasure without the arbitrary principles and conventional prohibitions, this behavior [incest] would not be condemned but would be tolerated as an extension of "the legitimate exercise of the sexual sense for its own ends. . . ." [207]

> That some children have been traumatized by brutal sexual assaults is a tragic truth, yet other children have looked back on early sexual experiences with high regard for the gentle and tender initiation to sexuality. We must avoid the judgments that speak of incest as "universally forbidden, by even the most backward people." [208]

## 2. Youth and Sex

> In our view, the taboos on premarital sex arose, historically, because pregnancy out of wedlock created problems for family organization, inheritance patterns, etc. Near-perfect contraception will change this, so that taboos on premarital intercourse are logical anachronisms. (The same logic might apply to incest and to some extent to adultery.) [209]

## 3. Bestiality

> Humanistic ethics include the primacy of human over subhuman sex goals, desires, and satisfactions. If lower animals are employed, for example, for purposes of bestiality, for the obtaining of sex hormones or stimulants, or for other purposes, this is normally an ethical pursuit of man. [210]

## 4. Homosexuality

> [T]here is no evidence at all that sexual preference of adults in the home has any detrimental impact on children. [M]ost children raised in [a] homosexual situation become heterosex-

ual as adults. . . . There is no evidence that children who are raised with a loving couple of the same sex are any more disturbed, unhealthy, [or] maladjusted than children raised with a loving couple of mixed sex.[211]

## 5. Adultery

In the studies and counseling experience of many, including ourselves, there is no evidence that all extra-marital sexual experience is destructive of the marriage. Indeed, more and more persons testify that creative co-marital relationships and sexual experience can and do exist.[212]

The eroticization of our culture oozes from its every pore, so much so that it becomes essentially absurd to expect that all physical sexual expression for a 50-year period will be confined to the marriage partner.[213]

## 6. Pornography

Whatever harm might be accomplished by pornography—and in individual cases it is hardly possible to deny such harm—there is some good to society by its dissemination; and some hurt to individuals, the social order, and to human freedom and aspirations by anti-pornography. Of the former, the social good of pornography, it acts as a force demanding greater self-reflection from within society, creating a counterculture to the staid, puritanical, and taken-for-granted world. It is a call for sexual revaluation, and that means that it is a force against stagnation and conservativism. As for the hurt, the suppression of pornography results in the establishment of a great force of law enforcement agents, self-appointed or government-appointed, as morals defenders, who are to state what reading and looking can be corrupting to others, although they are themselves immune from corruption by the same exposure. It is an unnecessary restraint upon freedom of expression, artistic and inartistic.[214]

## 7. General Nihilism

[F]or a considerable time to come, it is unlikely that rape, sexual murder, or an adult's taking advantage of a young child will be considered a perfectly justifiable and ethical act.[215]

A person would better try to have sex love relations in the here and now and to enthusiastically enjoy many immediate or short-range sexual pursuits; but he'd also better keep an eye on tomorrow and give up some immediate sex-love gains for longer range, future satisfactions. This means that, first, the individual is often wiser if he gives up present erotic pleasures for future erotic pleasures. Thus, he may. . . refrain from having intercourse with a minimum of foreplay in order to enjoy longer-lasting and deeper gratifications by employing more foreplay; [216]

Human beings should learn to appreciate and savor the immediacy of the Now;[217]

The tragic results of the influence from these abuses of our sexual ethics is detailed in Chapter I and are readily apparent to those who open their eyes. Senator Jeremiah Denton (R-Ala.) observed the devastating effects results of the sexual revolution after returning to the states from an absence of several years. Prior to his election to public office, Senator Denton spent seven and a half years in a North Vietnamese prison after being shot down while on a military mission. The only way his wife and seven children were sure he was alive was when he appeared on a North Vietnamese propaganda film on the treatment of prisoners of war. He risked his life to inform the nation of the North Vietnamese cruelty. While being interviewed on the propaganda film, Senator Denton blinked out the word "t-o-r-t-u-r-e" in Morse code. His safe return vaulted him to national prominence. The moral degeneration he observed upon his return spurred him to run for the U.S. Senate where he serves as the first Republican from Alabama in more than 160 years.[218]

His first action in the Senate was to introduce the Adolescent Family Life Bill, to help reverse America's immorality. At first no one took Senator Denton seriously. His bill was ridiculed as "the Chastity Bill." "But the tenacious freshman senator refused to give up,"[219] and finally achieved passage in Congress. Senator Denton wrote in the *Washington Post* that "millions of dollars have purchased America's adolescents sex education, contraceptives, and abortion counseling, without the knowledge or consent of parents. A new morality is always implicit and sometimes explicit in this policy: it teaches that sexual activity among teenagers is inevitable and acceptable so long as pregnancy does not result."[220]

As demonstrated by the quotes in "Incest" above, a frightening aspect of the sexual revolution is the advocacy of pedophilic rights. "They claim that present-day children are so isolated from warm, touching family relationships that incest is better than no intimacy at all."[221] One group which advocates the "new morality" is the Rene Guyon Society. Based in California, it claims to have 8,500 members who are avowed pedophiles and have as their motto: "Sex by eight is too late."[222] There exist many other similar groups such as the North American Man/Boy Love Association, etc.[223]

The book *Show Me*, which was written by a medical doctor and purports to be a sex education text suitable for seven and eight-year-olds, contains photographs which show sexual intercourse between young teenagers. It is also clear from the text that many of the couples engaged in coitus are not married. *Show Me* also depicts certain abnormal sex acts such as fellatio.[224] Seven and eight-year-olds have no interest or business in studying these acts. We are merely destroying childhood in the name of "enlightened education." The sexual revolution has radically altered the whole fabric of our society. There are almost no limitations to our conduct. Permissiveness is elevated: discipline and restraint are debased. Our society searches not for happiness but for immediate genital gratification.

The urges and instincts to reproduce and rear posterity can have a powerfully cohesive effect on communities and be a major force for the positive development of the individual. When properly employed, these urges can strengthen love and unity within the family, induce responsibility in the youth and help establish goals and cause the community to give thought and concern to the future. When abused, these urges can destroy a society as surely as they can perpetuate it. A relaxed moral standard engenders a concentration on self-gratification by any and all means. A high moral standard encourages strong family ties, both laterally and horizontally, and thus a pride in heritage and racial identity. One major reason that the white race did not mix with the Indians in the colonies was that the Puritans' strict moral code and values prohibited it. Early colonial law incorporated the death penalty of the Bible for adultery with either English or Indian. This strict penalty, however, was rarely, if ever, enforced[225] and was later reduced. Our countrymen retained their white heritage because of this value system. We have lost those values and are now becoming a colored people.

Conventional Christian morality has taught us that sexual transgressions are next to murder in seriousness. Our forefathers embraced that principle; our contemporaries scoff at it. Societies through the ages have seen the various manifestations and methods of destruction brought about by sexual abuses and so have developed a code of morality to avoid such occurrences. If we continue to disregard this code of morality, our nation will decline and ultimately collapse.

In support of incest, anthropologists cite the resulting "strength of the Ptolemies of Egypt or the Incas of Peru"[226] who alledgedly practiced it. Anthropologists of tomorrow studying a dead America, or even foreign anthropologists studying our culture today, could very well conclude that we practice incest. Is this the reputation we want to achieve? In support of adultery, anthropologists cite various societies which allegedly permit it: "Baiga, Copper Eskimo, Fiji, Kwoma, Lepcha, Lesu, Marquesas, Morngin, Puka-Puka, Siriono, Siwai and Toda"[227] Assuming that the assertions of these anthropologists are correct, does America want to be included among the ranks of these primitive and inconsequential societies?

The research and findings of anthropologists and sociologists have become suspect in recent years. It is now being discovered that many of them went into primitive cultures and social situations with preconceived notions and beliefs and then set about with their biases accumulating, and at times fabricating, data which supported their positions and overlooking data which did not. Most notable of the suspect anthropologists is Margaret Mead and her book *The Coming of Age in Samoa.*[228]

It is incumbent on today's citizen to look at most surveys, studies and reports with a discerning eye. Most researchers and writers have biases and selfish purposes to achieve. When a sociologist or anthropologist, in order to support such destructive philosophies as sexual permissiveness, cites research that strains the credulity of the average person, such research should automatically become suspect. One example is research cited by Alfred C. Kinsey regarding non-marital sexual experience. Kinsey describes the sexual activity of the Lepchas of Sikkim, a Himalayan tribe, asserting that it is practically divorced from emotion, that, among them, it is much like food and drink, and like food and drink it does not matter from whom they receive it, so long as they receive it, although they are grateful to those who provide either to them regularly.[229] We should be extremely skeptical of such findings, particularly if they are used to tear down our moral structure.

Further, we should be skeptical when anthropologists and sociologists assert that: in seventeenth-century America and England, "English sex customs had developed in ways that created an especially heavy burden for females. Woman's status had reached new lows in history as women became property, prostitution flourished and chastity became something of a marketable commodity."[230] Large societies and cultures are wide and varied, so an anthropologist digging deep enough can uncover all types of scan-

dalous activities in his subject society. This does not, however, justify conclusions such as the one quoted above, particularly when it is used to assert
that strict sexual ethics are themselves "insane and immoral"[231] and that
a person should "enthusiastically enjoy many immediate or short-range sexual
pursuits."[232]

The laws of early England and America do not support the contention
of a notorious double standard or that "women's status had reached new
lows in history." First of all, if the sociologist and anthropologist quoted
above are referring to Elizabethan England, they should note that the supreme
ruler of the country was a woman, Queen Elizabeth, and following her from
1689-94, was another woman ruler, Queen Mary II. How can women be
"property" when a queen is ruler? Further, such characterizations do not
correspond with family records of the era, such as wills and probate court
records which indicate that distaff ancestors were virtual equals with their
husbands.[233] In the middle 1600s through the early 1700s, the period to which
the above-quoted expert is referring, the proponderance of adultery convictions in England appear to be against men, not women.[234] The early colonial American laws regarding adultery (such as Massachusetts adultery laws)
made by the Courte of Assistants, appear to be sexually neutral, punishing
both men and women with equal severity.[235]

Double sexual standards are not good or fair. In the past, in various cultures
of mankind they have existed and still exist today. They exist primarily
because societies recognize the need for a strong sexual ethic, but women,
more than men, are better at abiding by the higher standard, and men generally rule the societies. Men, therefore, at times, excuse their actions but do
not excuse their wives' actions. The double standards also exist to help ensure that the man is indeed the father of his wife's child, since she has control over that occurrence by her fidelity or infidelity.

Regardless of the inequities of a double standard, the solution is not to
even up the sexual standards between men and women by eliminating all
standards, but by assisting the lax standard to become more disciplined. Of
all the sexual standards, the one advocated and practiced by an America
influenced by the sexual revolution is the worst. A double standard requiring more discipline on the part of the woman is far better than the one we
have now because under a double standard at least half of society would
be constrained to be moral.

It is very important for America's well-being to reestablish traditional views
and standards regarding sexual ethics. We must strive to be disciplined, control our reproductive urges and channel them in proper directions. Chastity

should be something to strive to maintain. Because of consumer economics in our free-enterprise system human sexuality has become our most salable commodity. It needs to be deemphasized and made to be a more private issue. The eroticization of our culture must cease and our numb and jaded public needs to once again become offended at the offensive. The mass media which promotes this eroticization has such a profound influence on our society that the emasculated institutions which support our traditional values, such as schools, churches and homes, are unable to combat the onslaught. Curbs are necessary. The free-market system, freedom of speech and individual rights will survive curbs enacted by society to deemphasize sex, but none of these liberties, or our society itself, can survive the result of continued decadence.

Homosexuality is not "good " or "beautiful" or even "victimless". It is an unnatural act that tears down society, whether conducted in public or private. Yet, the sad trend is that homosexuality is gaining acceptance, and the average American is becoming so jaded that he is no longer even able to recognize its ill effects.

In our society, acts of beastiality, homosexuality, incest, pedophilia, adultery, fornication, viewing pornography, and abortion, are enacted millions upon millions of times. Do we want our society to be characterized by these customs and traits? Does America want its beacon of freedom to be blackened in support of these unsupportable deviations? Why will we not instill in our children a pride in being chaste? Why do we permit countless incidents of eroticization to confront us each day? Why do we condone sexual activity outside the bonds of marriage? Why do we so want to save baby seals, but so want to destroy human embryos?

Most of us know what is right and wrong. All we must do is admit it and then strive to do what is right. The nice thing about life and society is that each generation brings new innocence and hope. Our little children can always be moral and, as adults, can experience the joy of a private and monogamous relationship if we afford them that chance; not by teaching them about oral sex and adultery at age seven and eight as the health text *Show Me* does, but by reestablishing our values and protecting our charges from the evils of our generation.

As will be discussed below, we can accomplish this change in our society by reexamining our political structure and returning to the system of federalism and the checks and balances established by our Founding Fathers. We are yet a prosperous nation, and prosperity breeds complacency. A complacent America and a divided America, which we are also, cannot easily become motivated enough or united enough to force a bulky, powerful central government to effect the changes necessary to provide our children with the type of society they deserve. Accordingly, the solution advocated by this author is to redilute the federal government's power by reempowering the states with rights not delegated to the federal government by means of a justly interpreted constitution. The states and communities would then be empowered to institute certain curbs they deem necessary to preserve our traditional values, and the citizenry could then effect those curbs through modest campaigning on their part.

## (c) Standards of Conduct Concerning the Community

### (i) Religion

Man, being an intelligent agent, acts with a view to an end. His whole life and his actions are ordered toward this end. Men adopt different methods of proceeding toward their proposed ends, as the diversity of their pursuits clearly indicates.[236] Consequently, man needs directive principles to help him decide on the end he proposes and to guide him in his efforts to achieve that end.

Traditionally, both our individual and national ends and our principles have been heavily influenced by the Bible and Christianity. The Bible has provided us with our sense of morality and has helped us define right and wrong conduct. At the outset of this nation, worship of God and living this life with a view to an eternal reward was our premier end to pursue. Second to that end was our desire for personal freedom and liberty. Through the years, the order of these two ends, worship of God and personal liberty, became reversed. At first, religion in America was such an important end that the concepts of individual freedom, as well as other principles, suffered. However, as religious fervor subsided in the American colonies, the importance of individual freedom evolved and grew until it became a more important end than religion. Its importance continued to grow and religion continued to wane until we have come to see the concepts of individual liberty in America overwhelm and stifle the ends of religion, as well as other ends. Hence, today we have an exact reverse of America's Puritan era.

This is a natural and logical evolution in that, in many senses, religion, as an end, highlights certain principles that personal liberty, as an end, supresses, and personal liberty, as an end, highlights certain principles that religion supresses. Religion, as an end, generally promotes discipline and conformity to structured dogma and tenets. It promotes a unity in people, culture and beliefs. It tends to be doctrinaire and dictatorial. Religion teaches that principles are more important than life itself and often promotes the parish over the individual. Where religion as an end tends to be doctrinaire and dictatorial, individual liberty, taken to an extreme, tends to support anarchy and division. It promotes the individual over the group and the individual over principles. Where religion promotes discipline and conformity to structured dogma, individual liberty provides for an escape from discipline, a breakdown of structured dogma and morals and a diversity in culture and heritage.

It is often said by sociologists that in a backward or developing society, religion plays an important role in the everyday lives of the individual.[237] When life is harsh, the people in the society look to a future state when life will be blissful. Conversely, an advanced society tends to reject religion as "an opiate of the people."[238] This proclivity in the advanced nations to move away from religion is bolstered by the fact that a religious life is a more disciplined, and therefore harder, existence. It is the nature of man to move toward the easier, less disciplined lifestyle, if he can find justification therefore. Since a wealthy society often feels it does not need religious discipline, and since its lifestyle tends toward the easy and pleasureable path and away from the strict and ascetic path, it is a natural course that America takes when it switches its end from strict religion to extreme liberty as its fortunes improve.

In order to demonstrate this change in our life's end from religion to individual liberty, I think that it would be useful to cite various historical documents which recite these ends or goals. The Mayflower Compact of November ll, l620, reveals that the first colonists to America maintained as their end "the Glory of God and Advancement of the Christian Faith, and the Honor of [their] King and Country." In furtherance of the aforesaid ends, those colonists "solomnly and mutually in the Presence of God and one another, covenant[ed] and combine[d them]selves together into a civil Body Politick," and "enact[ed], constitute[d] and frame[d] just and equal Laws, Ordinances, Acts, Constitutions and Offices."[239]

The Maryland Toleration Act of l649 reveals that the colonists felt that "Fforasmuch as in a well governed and Christian Common Wealth matters concerning Religion and the honor of God ought in the first place to bee taken into serious consideration and endeavoured to bee settled."

Therefore they enacted,"that whatsoever person or persons within the Province... shall from henceforth blaspheme God... or shall deny our Saviour Jesus Christ to bee the sonne of God, or shall deny the holy Trinity the ffather, sonne and holy Ghost, or the Godhead... shall be punished with death and confiscation or forfeiture of all his or her lands. And (except as in this present Act is before Declared and sett forth) that noe person or persons . . . professing to believe in Jesus Christ, shall from henceforth bee any weiss troubled, molested or discountenanced for or in respect of his or her religion nor in the free exercise thereof . . . . "[240]

These two documents demonstrate the importance of religion in early America's life. One hundred twenty-seven years later, stress on individual liberty is apparent. The Virginia Bill of Rights of June 12, 1776, provides that "all men are by nature equally free and independent, and have certain inherent rights . . . namely, the enjoyment of life, liberty, with the means of acquiring and possessing property, and pursuing and obtaining happiness and safety," and that "religion, or the duty which we owe to our Creator . . . can be directed only by reason and conviction, not by force or violence . . . and that it is the mutual duty of all to practice Christian forebearance, love, and charity towards each other."[241]

Further, the Massachusetts Bill of Rights of 1780 provided that: "all men are born free and equal, and have certain natural, essential, and unalienable rights; among which may be reckoned the right of enjoying and defending their lives and liberties; that of acquiring, possessing, and protecting property; in fine, that of seeking and obtaining their safety and happiness." It further provides that:

"It is the right as well as the duty of all men in society, publicly, and at stated seasons, to worship the Supreme Being, the great Creator and Preserver of the universe. And no subject shall be hurt, molested, or restrained in his person, liberty, or estate, for worshipping God in the manner and season most agreeable to the dictates of his own conscience; or for his religious profession of sentiments; provided he doth not disturb the public peace, or obstruct others in their religious worship . . . .

"As the happiness of a people and the good order and preservation of civil government essentially depend upon piety, religion, and morality, and as these cannot be generally diffused through a community but by the institution of the public worship of God and of public instructions, in piety, religion, and morality. Therefore to promote their happiness and secure the good order and preservation of their government, the people of this commonwealth have a right to invest their legislature with power to authorize and require, and the legislature shall from time to time authorize and require, the several towns... and other bodies-politic or religious societies, to make suitable provision, at their own expense, for the institution of the public worship of God and the support and maintenance of public Protestant teachers of piety, religion, and morality . . . .

"And every denomination of Christians, demeaning themselves peaceably and as good subjects of the commonwealth, shall be equally under the protection of the law; and no subordination of any one sect or denomination to another shall ever be established by law."[242]

An elevation of liberty is indicated by the preamble to the Constitution which provides that: "We the people of the United States, in order to . . . promote the general welfare, and secure the blessings of liberty to ourselves and our posterity, do ordain and establish this Constitution for the United States of America."[243]

In contrast to the emphasis on religion as evidenced by most of the above quotes, Secretaty of State George Shultz stated as follows in his address at the 86th Annual Washington Day Banquet on February 22, 1984:[244]

"Unlike most other nations, we are not defined by an ancient common tradition or heritage or by ethnic homogeneity. Unlike most other countries, America is a nation consciously created and made up of men and women from many different cultures and origins. What unifies us is not a common origin but a common set of ideals: freedom, constitutional democracy, racial and religious tolerance. We Americans thus define ourselves not by where we come from but by where we are headed: our goals, our values, our principles, which mark the kind of society we strive to create.

"This accounts in good part, I believe, for the extraordinary vitality of this country. Democracy is a great liberator of the human spirit, giving free rein to the talents and aspirations of individuals, offering every man and woman the opportunity to realize his or her fullest potential. This ideal of freedom has been a beacon to immigrants from many lands."

When our society had as its primary end, the worship of God and living life with a view to an eternal reward, the principles of morality and Christian teachings were the most important guidelines in our lives. Individual freedom was always important to us, but the principles and beliefs furthering this end were generally secondary to the religious ones. As individual liberty and freedom became more valued ends than religious tenets, the principles and beliefs supporting it became more important and influential in our lives, and in times of conflict between the two ends the principles of individual liberty prevailed.

By our Christian teachings and heritage we can discern the evil and destructive nature of pornography, homosexuality, adultery, divorce, drug abuse, lying, cheating, allowing the guilty to escape punishment, miscegination, illegal immigration, etc. However, our proposed end of individual liberty taken to its current extreme constrains us from taking effective measures to eliminate and cure these threats to our morality and heritage. Currently, our beliefs as to the importance of the freedom of the press and freedom of speech outweigh our concerns for propriety and propagation of chastity and fidelity. Our beliefs as to the individual's rights to engage in immoral, irresponsible and undisciplined acts are more influential than our commitment to one another to maintain a strong, healthy society. Our beliefs as to the rights of the nonwhites and recent immigrants are more influential in shaping our conduct than our innate desire to preserve our own territory, people, culture and heritage.

The problems with our attitudes toward religion are twofold. The first problem is a personal one. Many of us either no longer believe in God or religion or do not stand up in support of our beliefs. The second problem is a legal one. The federal courts in their rulings over the years have interpreted the U.S. Constitution in such a manner as to frustrate religious belief and to foster disbelief.[245] In short, today's government takes a hostile view toward religion. Religion is an essential element for the preservation and advancement of our society. As mentioned earlier, traditionally, religion was the reason Americans established as their primary end progression and improvement for themselves and their posterity. The impetus behind the original colonization of America was Christianity and freedom of worship. The early settlers maintained strong and sincere belief in God, with a steadfast commitment to the principles of integrity and uprightness that arise therefrom. They believed this was the basis for enabling man to become a superior being. Belief in God and the concept that God had given the land to the Colonists helped influence the manner in which our forefathers fashioned the framework of this nation. One result of the deemphasis of religion in our society is the elimination of a major impetus to do good and commit oneself to principles of integrity and uprightness. As long as the tenets of our religion required us to be honest, chaste and industrious and we believed that our eternal happiness depended upon adherence to those tenets, we were motivated and disposed to acquire those traits, whereas, the substitution as our primary end in life of worshipping God and living life with the view to an eternal reward with maximum individual liberty and freedom is a major factor in our "me-generation" quest for self-gratification and indulgence. When we switched our primary end in life from living religious tenets to expanding our individual liberty and freedom, to a certain extent, we stopped progressing on a vertical level, i.e. building for the future generations and improving ourselves in order to attain ultimate happiness through religious exhaltation, and we began expanding on horizontal levels i.e., seeking pleasure and fulfillment through wide and varied experiences which do not elevate but only gratify.

Irrespective of the arguments in support of or against the existence of God or the truthfulness of the Christian religion (or any other religion for that matter), it being a part of the Divine Plan that proof of said things be unattainable, religion and belief in God serve a vital purpose in the American culture, which is to urge man to progress vertically and improve all aspects of his life in a manner consonant with America's traditional values.

As the facts and statistics of Chapter I indicate, many of us have rejected our religious beliefs in recent years and have even assumed the opposite posture that belief in God limits freedom, is un-American and destructive. Those who profess a belief in God and advocate others to do likewise, such as the Evangelical Christians, are often called "despotic" and "fascist."[246] As a result, many of the most outspoken Christians are cowed from vocally advocating morality and religion. American societal pressure often prevents us from promulgating morality for fear of restricting the freedom of the unbeliever. Moreover, because of an extreme liberalization in our interpretations of constitutional rights, the courts have taken a hostile posture towards religion and have made it illegal in many instances for society to encourage belief in God.[247] This breakdown in belief in God and the rejection of the accompanying methods of worship contributes to our moral decay and allows us to substitute uplifting precepts and practices with ideology and practices that tear down instead of build. We deceive ourselves into thinking that our country will not suffer because of this change. We think that we can remain a strong nation without religion and a strong code of morals to instill our citizens with honesty, trust, unity, a clear identity of our past and concern for the future. Regardless of all the bad that has been said about religion, belief in God will help us to perceive right from wrong and commitment to the tenets of worship will enable us to carry out our convictions.

A major factor in the emasculation of religion as the bulwark of morality is the current interpretation the courts have placed on the religious guarantees of the first amendment to the Constitution. The amendment expresses the basic and sound concept that Congress shall make no law establishing a religion or prohibiting the free exercise thereof. It should be noted that these provisions of the first amendment initially applied only to the federal government and not to the states. Formerly, actions by the states were governed in this regard only by what was provided in their own respective constitutions. Now, however, the due process clause of the fourteenth amendment has been extended to make the first amendment apply to state action as well. This legal development will be explained in detail later because it is an issue central to this text.

It is this principle of freedom of worship that we want to maintain in our country. However, over the years, our courts and legal scholars have taken this basic principle and modified it and expounded on it and have blown it out of proportion. As a result, instead of merely avoiding the tyranny of a state religion, which was the purpose of the amendment, we have a government that frustrates society from passing its religion and code of morality on to its posterity.

No well society would construct so many obstacles to impede the indoctrination of values into the rising generation as our nation has done. No nation before us has ever weakened itself so soundly by rejecting the heritage, values and beliefs that gave it strength as we are doing now. The irony of it all is that we are doing it in the name of democracy and liberty. For three hundred and fifty years our ancestors prayed in schools. Then in 1962-1963 in *Engel v. Vitale*[248] and *Abington School District v. Schampp*,[249] the landmark school prayer and Bible-reading decisions, the U.S. Supreme Court rejected that tradition and method of indoctrinating our youth in principles of reverence and morality.

It is important to keep the doctrine of freedom of religion in perspective. The Founding Fathers never meant the first amendment guarantees to be used to thwart religious and cultural indoctrination as the U.S. Supreme Court has been doing since the school-prayer and Bible-reading decisions. Where, in 1952, the U.S. Supreme Court in *Zorach v. Clauson*[250] acknowledged the religious nature of the citizenry and said that it was consistent with the best national tradition to accommodate public religious service to fit spiritual needs, today, it appears to be the view that any governmental purpose to advance religion generally, such as through the erection, maintenance or display of religious structures or symbols on public property, constitutes a violation of religious freedom.[251]

In addition, the Founding Fathers never intended the First Amendment to be used to allow the substitution of this country's Christian culture, morality and heritage in favor of other religions and cultures. The word "religion" is not defined in the Constitution. In order to ascertain its meaning, one must refer to other sources, and no source is more appropriate than the history of the period during which the provision for the protection of religious liberty was adopted. The courts have held that "religion" does not mean only the "Christian religion."[252] And that "although, as distinguished from the religions of Confucius, Gautama, Mohammed, or even Abraham, it was early said that by reason of the number, influence, and station of its devotees within the United States, the religion of Christ is the prevailing religion of this country."[253] The Court said "with equal truth it may be said that, from the dawn of civilization, the religion of a country is a most important factor in determining its form of government, and that stability of government in no small measure depends upon the reverence and respect which a nation maintains toward its prevalent religion."[254]

Our nation should certainly allow religious freedom, but it should not carry that doctrine to such an extreme that in its efforts to protect the emotions of the minority the rights of the majority suffer. A Buddhist or an atheist could still have the freedom to worship, or not worship, even though the school his child attends prays a Christian prayer and his courthouse displays a creche. A Muslim would still have religious freedom even though his child's school district provides time release programs to accommodate Christian seminary and bible study programs, but does not accommodate eight daily prayers to Allah. A Sikh could still be a Sikh even though the Army demands he remove his turban and beard yet allows a Catholic to wear a cross or a Mormon his temple garments.

Our country is a Christian nation in religion, morals and culture. Allowing freedom of religion does not mean undermining our way of life. The Sihk, Muslim or Buddhist should expect to conform to the Christian majority when living in a Christian country. The nation should not be required to sacrifice its way of life to accommodate the customs and rites of the minority. It should allow freedom of religion to non-Christians and accommodate them wherever practical and non-burdensome but no more. Otherwise, our nation will undermine our way of life for a principle taken to an extreme.

Until World War II, the U.S. Supreme Court had little involvement in the church and state doctrine.[255] After the Second World War, the U.S. Supreme Court implicitly began to adopt the idea that a democratic government needed to be protected against the encroachments of religious zealotry.[256] "A study of the postwar litigation up to 1971 shows that [anti-religious bias of the court] came about primarily because of a determination on the part of certain interested organizations to raise basic philosophical and constitutional issues, and, through litigation, force resolution of these matters. The manifest liberalism of the Warren Court particularly encouraged such suits."[257] "The modern Court has been vigilant in excluding from public support activities that are traditionally recognized as religious, almost all of them Christian in character."[258] The U.S. Supreme Court's "neutral stance" is in fact disparaging to religious views.[259]

The solution to the Court's hostility toward religion might be to return to the situation existing before World War II when the Court had little involvement in the church and state doctrine. Communities would then be free to strike their own balance between church and state. The method of achieving this will be set forth further below.

### (ii) Crime

There exists in the United States a broad and distinct division on how to best address the problems of crime. Whether the topic for discussion is mandatory prison sentences for serious offenders, capital punishment, youth crime policy or police use of deadly force, it appears that the same type of people are consistently at odds.[260] Frequently, this division is characterized as a struggle between liberal and conservative ideologies.[261] The liberals tend to view the origins of crime as institutional, noting elements which transcend the individual criminal. They mention such factors as poverty, unemployment, lack of opportunity, racism, broken homes, and peer group pressure.

Conservatives often speak in terms of selfishness, lack of discipline, lack of respect for and fear of the law, and the general evil to which feral men are disposed. President Richard Nixon, a proponent of the conservative view on criminal justice, denied that the criminal is not responsible for his crimes against society. During his presidency he stated, "Society is guilty only when we fail to bring the criminal to justice."[262] Further, other conservatives argue that those who believe that bad social institutions corrupt naturally good men ignore the possibility that naturally bad men corrupt good institutions.[263]

According to Robert Mortinson, many "liberal" criminologists in recent years are likely to do "everything in their power to ridicule the very idea of deterrence."[264] As an alternative to punitive measures, "liberals" are likely to recommend "therapeutic" treatment of offenders rather than "punishment."[265] Hard-line "conservatives" often regard criminals as a class apart from the rest of society. As James O. Wilson puts it, there are "the wicked" and "the innocent."[266]

The facts and evidence supporting the separate liberal and conservative ideolgies on crime control are lacking on both sides.[267] Conservatives argue that the death penalty is a deterrent and that the "professional law enforcement officer is convinced from experience that the hardened criminal has been and is deterred from killing based on the prospect of the death penalty."[268] Liberals, on the other hand (such as Sing Sing's Warden Kirchwey) state:

> [Punishment] cannot deter the mentally defective, they cannot appreciate their danger. It cannot deter the insane, their minds are too distorted to reason. It cannot deter the antisocial, they

are at war with society and the danger but gives pleasing zest
to the contest. It cannot deter the thoughtful and deliberate, for
they have no intention of getting caught. Nor can it deter the
impulsive, for impulse is always quicker than reason.[269]

In the liberal-conservative debate over approaches to control crime, the
facts, evidence and theories are bandied about with equal ferociousness on
either side, yet neither side's arguments have proved convincing or successful
enough to bring about a cure. If the solution were readily apparent or easily
reached, there would not be such a debate over the two ideologies. Much
of the ideological differences are based on procedural measures, safeguards
and theory in solving crime that have only marginal differences in degrees
of extremeness. The debate over capital punishment, a matter of life and
death, is not even an area where the differences between liberal and conservative are extreme because capital punishment is meted out so rarely, that
whether it occurs only to a small number of felons or does not occur at
all has little effect on society at large.

In recent years, the liberals have consistently won the procedural battles
in the courts. Particularly, the 1960s registered a series of landmark U.S.
Supreme Court decisions expanding the due process concepts to enlarge the
rights to criminal defendants.[270] Under the liberal Warren Court, interpretations of the fourteenth amendment and the bill of rights by a consensus of
activist justices resulted in expanding the rights of criminals in such areas
as the fourth amendment protection against search and seizures, the fifth
amendment right against self-incrimination and the sixth amendment right
to counsel and trial by jury.[271] These rights had been expanded for the criminal
in the federal courts but were expanded by the Warren court to include the
state court system as well.[272]

The Warren court established the exclusionary rule in *Mapp v. Ohio*[273]
which forbids the use of any evidence in state criminal trials that was seized
in violation of the Court's interpretation of the technical requirements of
the fourth amendment search and seizure provision. The Burger court has
carved out various exceptions to this rule to emasculate its devastating effect on law enforcement but has not overturned it.[274] Judges and legal scholars
have long been opposed to the exclusionary rule on the ground that it has
little or no effect in halting illegal police conduct but does allow the guilty
to go free because of police bungling.[275]

In *Miranda v. Arizona*,[276] the U.S. Supreme Court held that police must
inform suspects in custody of their right to remain silent, of the right to
counsel and to appointed counsel if they are indigent and the fact that any

statement they made could be held against them. If police obtain statements in technical violation of this rule, they must be suppressed and cannot be used at trial.[277] The U.S. Supreme Court, under Warren Burger has limited the scope of the *Miranda* ruling, but it still acts as an impediment to justice of the people against its malefactors.[278]

As for the U.S. Supreme Court's interpretation of the fifth amendment right to jury, the U.S. Supreme Court overturned the conviction of a Mexican-American who was convicted of burglary of a private residence with intent to rape because the ratio of minority group members on the Texas Grand Jury was disproportionately lower than their ratio to the general population.[279] Further, in 1972, the U.S. Supreme Court in the case of *Furman v. Georgia*,[280] struck down as unconstitutional the state laws permitting capital punishment. This ruling was based on the eighth amendment prohibition of cruel and unusual punishment. States have had to rewrite their criminal codes to limit capital punishment to a narrow range of murder applied in a manner the U.S. Supreme Court views as being non-arbitrary.[281] With regard to state prison facilities, federal courts have intervened to prohibit states from carrying out sentences on the convicted prisoners when lack of funds prohibit states from providing for the burgeoning number of criminals in areas of adequate medical care, sanitary facilities, lack of physical exercise, loss of contact with family and overcrowding.[282] Federal courts have intervened to establish a detailed constitutional code of prison administration.[283] The U.S. Supreme Court held that states had to provide convicted criminals with law libraries, no matter what the cost.[284] In *Wolff v. McDonnell*[285] the U.S. Supreme Court held that an unruly prisoner subject to discipline was entitled to a hearing with due process safeguards.

In spite of the liberal philosophies behind the above rulings, justice is not served by letting the guilty go free or unpunished. We must elevate the rights of society and the law-abiding individual over those of the criminal. "[I]n this world, as it is, justice may need to be secured by force; failure to attempt to resist by force the depredations of invaders, pirates, and recalcitrants will normally be a failure in justice."[286]

Clear solutions to the problems of our criminal justice system are unavailable. Reacting to the problem of crime with a demand for swift, extreme punishment seems simplistic. "A myriad of intervening factors lie between the death penalty on the law books and criminal acts on the street."[287] A U.S. Supreme Court ruling upholding capital punishment, by itself, is likely to have little impact on the rate of serious criminal offenses.

To be effective, punishment must be enforced. The laws and the courts must punish criminals. Empirical facts indicate a leniency in applying the law. When an overwhelming majority of convicted felons are not punished for their acts but are released to society, they are allowed to further perpetrate crimes by their own actions and their example of non-punishment to other potential offenders.

Mercy also has its place in our criminal system, but mercy must come after justice is served. Otherwise, the just are mocked and the morale of society declines. Mercy should be granted to the criminal after retribution has been made. When a criminal has suffered for his crime, then it is the duty of society to accept him, show mercy upon him and help him become a productive citizen. Justice is not served when crimes go unpunished or when punishments are not fit for the crime (when they are either too lenient or too harsh), or when prisons resemble recreation facilities more than they do institutions of punishment. Our society must have a program for rehabilitation which is in addition to, and not in place of, punishment. Otherwise there is no justice. Even if the criminal reforms under rehabilitation programs (an unlikely possibility) but is not punished for his crime, justice will not be met, and the consequence thereof is the weakening of society.

The major object of penal servitude should not be deterrence of the criminal. Deterrence should be achieved by other means such as social and community influence and elevated standards of conduct instilled in the individual by the family. The major objective of penal servitude and capital punishment is serving justice. No matter what the researchers try to show, crime may not decrease even when justice is served, but crime will certainly not decrease when justice is not served. Mercy to the criminal sentenced to long-term imprisonment or to execution is in teaching him and those he influences about justice. There is no mercy in allowing the convicted felon to go unpunished because he does not learn justice and thus, can never adjust to society and its demands.

A possible substantive law solution to the crime problem would be to remove the U.S. Supreme Court's jurisdiction over the bulk of the criminal field as was once the case, and reempower the states with the right to institute exact punishments without the interference of a contradictory and far-removed federal government. States would, once again, then be free to institute measures that they feel are necessary to preserve and protect their communities from the criminal element. The arguments in favor of reempowering the states with the right to criminal law decision-making are set forth further below.

### (iii) Drug Abuse

Nancy Reagan, in her drive against drug abuse, visited an adolescent drug-treatment center early in 1984. She met a pretty eleven-year-old child who had just completed treatment. Mrs. Reagan asked when the little girl had begun using drugs and the youngster replied, "I was two months old." Her parents had put alcohol and drugs in her baby bottle to keep her quiet. By age six, she began smoking marijuana, and by age ten, she had resorted to prostitution to support her habit.[288]

Ghetto children and children of presidential hopefuls alike, destroy their futures and their lives with drugs. Our laws do not demand vigorous action to curb this threat to our society. The enforcement arm of the government is not able to use the laws that exist to curb the abuse. Society does not demand compliance with the drug enforcement laws or successfully condemn the drug trade. Drug abuse is another factor undermining the vitality and progress of America. How can America compete with Japan and other drug-free nations when our youth are wasting away using drugs supplied by a permissive society and condoned by a misconception of freedom?

Each social ill that America faces today—drugs, immorality, broken homes, illiteracy, idleness, diluted work ethic, racial strife, and inefficient yet over-reaching government—has a grossly detrimental effect on the well-being of our nation. This generation must confront each of these problems and solve them or the future of our society will be further imperiled. The method by which our society handles its drug problem is a prime example of our permissiveness and excesses. Our communities must once again establish their high moral principles and demand compliance thereto.

Through a lenient system, our society is more cruel and barbaric to allow Robert Kennedy's son, John Belushi and thousands of others to kill themselves with drugs or parents to destroy their children, like the eleven-year-old girl of Nancy Reagan's acquaintance, than for society to take swift and immediate action to curb drug abuse. It would be better to execute the convicted drug dealer than allow him to corrupt an entire generation. I do not mean to advocate such harsh measures. Less extreme approaches on the state and local levels might be enough to solve the problem. Nevertheless, effective measures, whatever they are, must be imposed or our nation will not survive.

Our criminal system has become so bulky and so ineffective that our current drug laws and enforcement agencies are unable to solve the drug abuse problem. States and communities must once again be empowered to effectively regulate the crimes its citizens perpetrate upon themselves and others. The bulky centralized system of government must be unwound and the rights reserved to the states must be returned to them. In this manner, the states and communities can enact and adopt curative measures for its social ills without an inefficient, misguided central government preventing reform. This method will be set forth further below.

### (iv) Entertainment

America's creative minds have been of the opinion that slang, profanity, oaths against Deity and general sloppiness are somehow more creative, artistic and real than propriety, reverence and comeliness. Hence, movie scripts no longer have the young heroine speak properly—instead she uses gutter language. Further, her elocution on film is so casual and garbled "for the sake of art and realism" that the audience must spend the entire movie straining to hear her subtly influence them to abandon refinement. Much of the popular music of today is not of an uplifting or refined character but is savage and nihilistic.

Where is the child going to learn manners, discipline, order and respect, if, in the name of liberty, his home is broken because both parents decide not to accept the responsibility of rearing him together; if, in the name of progressive education, his school teaches him he need not work hard to learn; and if, in the name of art, the movies and music set examples of profanity, poor manners and coarseness?

A major step in elevating our standards of conduct is to take measures to eliminate human sexuality as America's most saleable commodity in our entertainment industry. Congress and the state legislatures are severely restricted in enacting legislation to this end, primarily because the U.S. Supreme Court has basically extended the concept of free speech to protect from censorship all types of pornography and sexually prurient material except those that fall within an extremely liberal interpretation of obscenity. With regard to the scope of regulating obscene material, the U.S. Supreme Court does not undertake to tell the states what they must do but rather undertakes to define the area in which a state is not free to restrict on obscenity grounds.[289] The U.S. Supreme Court established the *Roth* test[290] which required three elements to be present before a work could be banned as being obscene: it had to be established that (1) the dominant theme of the material taken as a whole appeals to prurient interest in sex; (2) the material is patently offensive because it affronts contemporary community standards relating to description or representation of sexual matters; and (3) the material is utterly without redeeming social value.

Under this test, a film portraying illicit and perverted sexual relations was not obscene;[291] picture books of naked women in lewd poses was held not to be obscene;[292] the magazine *Gent*, notwithstanding its numerous pictures of nude women and descriptions of sexual arousal and satisfaction was not obscene.[293] The practical result of this and other tests handed down by the U.S. Supreme Court is that communities can, in fact, ban very little sexually arousing material, and pornographers are free to peddle even clearly obscene or pedophilic material until they are apprehended and tried in court.

A solution to this problem would be to remove this liberal U.S. Supreme Court's jurisdiction over the obscenity test and allow the state legislatures to adopt their own standards, as used to be the case. States that want to restrict obscene literature more broadly than is now allowed by the U.S. Supreme Court could do so, other states could leave the standard as it is. If states were to have varying standards, the stricter states would exercise influence over the less strict states because publishers and movie producers would be forced by the economics of reaching a wider audience to meet the standards of as many states as possible.

### (v) Laws, Lawyers and Litigation.

As mentioned above, one result of the breakdown of our standards of conduct is an increase in the amount and complexity of laws and legal activity necessary to compensate for moral principles that have been abandoned. A brief look to Chapter I reveals the extent of the law and litigation explosion.

A litigious and excessively codified society creates a repressive and counterproductive atmosphere. Laws that were originally established to insure and extend individual freedom have the reverse effect of preventing individuals from exercising their fundamental rights. Due to the civil rights laws, school boards are often deterred or prohibited from dismissing both the incompetent teacher and the truly destructive one.[294] Employers are often deterred from applying reason and judgment in the employment process and instead reduce their hiring procedures to a system of quotas and progressive formulae which the employer may fear will result in an overall inefficiency in the marketplace.[295] Even if it does not, the fact that the employer cannot decide for himself is an indication of an absence of freedom to choose. Because of various municipal civil rights regulations, federal law and threats of litigation related thereto, religious groups and private and public employers are often constrained from denying employment to homosexuals even when the employer feels they are gross violators of their religious tenets.[296] For fear of public reprisals, lawsuits or government investigation, religious groups have stopped keeping records of divorce, church sanctions and other information that is vital to their adminstrative activities.[297] Churches are even being sued to prevent them from denouncing their members for immoral acts.[298] Businesses often decide not to enter into certain ventures because the extent of governmental control leaves it unclear as to whether or not their activities will be acceptable to government administrators.[299]

Excessive laws and litigation are a great inhibition on the freedom of the people and help make our businesses inefficient. The legal profession is a service industry that has grown out of our excess of laws and does not serve a valuable enough purpose to justify the millions of workers and trillions of dollars devoted to its perpetuation. The law and litigation explosion has already expanded beyond a healthy level. It is important for the efficient progression of our society to change our present course in this regard by eliminating much of the litigation and the need for such extensive laws.

If Americans once again governed themselves by their standards of conduct, the number and complexity of the laws would decrease. If people became more moral, the amount of contention and litigation would also decrease.[300]

Finally, our court system is too complex, providing too much legal redress and too many appeals for every conceivable civil injustice. Often the U.S. Supreme Court rules but does not guide.[301] When the U.S. Supreme Court is indecisive, litigation in the nation's courts multiplies. "Whenever a legal or constitutional issue is left unsettled, attorneys file new lawsuits in the hope that they will eventually prevail. And lower court judges, finding themselves unbound by any clear Supreme Court precedent, hand down a myriad of contradictory opinions as each individual jurist strives to interpret the ambiguities in the law."[302] A method of reducing the confusion of U.S. Supreme Court indecision and the injustice of the U.S. Supreme Court overreaching is the decentralization of legal decision-making, that is, by restrengthening the states' power to govern themselves.

As will be discussed in more detail in the states' rights section set forth further below, the framers of the Constitution established a limit to governmental control and authority by creating a dual or federal system by delegating to the central government only those powers which could not efficiently and conveniently be exercised locally.[303] Until this century, the states' exercise of regulation over the residuary areas not forbidden them by the U.S. Constitution, was almost unrestricted.[304] In consequence, the states were free to make innovations in both procedural and substantives law without review or restraints by the U.S. Supreme Court.[305]

It is through this method of localized decision-making that our nation can take action to unclog the courts and strip away certain laws and regulations that are counterproductive. If the local citizenry wanted to reduce the number of appeals and stalling tactics afforded to the criminal or litigious individuals, it could take such action on the local level and not be prevented by an over-reaching and contradictory U.S. Supreme Court. It is much easier for an individual to shape the laws that rule his life if the decision-making is done on a local level. If legislation is done on a national level, change by a community and by the entire country is difficult indeed to accomplish. Currently, the federal government sets the speed limits to which traffic shall proceed on every country lane throughout the nation.[306] It sets the standards for the composition of state juries, both grand and petit.[307] It requires the provision of defense counsel at state expense in an innumerable variety of cases where the enforcement of state laws or municipal ordinances may involve the possibility of imprisonment.[308] It prescribes the manner in which state elections are held and even requires the ballots to be printed in foreign languages.[309] As mentioned above, under the *Miranda* and other rulings, the federal government and the U.S. Supreme Court specify conditions under which interrogation of prisoners may be conducted[310] and requires the exclusion of evidence obtained in violation of these rules or other rules which the U.S. Supreme Court deduces in exact constitutional provisions.[311]

The central government causes much more injustice to society through allowing the guilty to go free as was ever allowed in other eras or nations under other theories and doctrines. Through the divisions and limitation of powers and by the localization of decision-making, which are inherent but disregarded in our federal system, the rights of the individual and the community can be best preserved and balanced with each other against the evils of concentrated centralized power, which history discloses as having always presaged the destruction of liberty.

### (d) Standards of Conduct Concerning Industry

Our country has lost much of the strictness and discipline that characterized us during our growth years. Strictness and discipline are virtues that are not highly valued in much of America today. We have ignored these principles in education, employment, punishment and even in our diet. A detrimentally large number of us believe that liberty means freedom from doing the unpleasant. Our children attend school for the fewest hours per day and for the fewest days per year of any developed nation.[312] Our workers have a reputation for low productivity and high absenteeism. Our retirement system often allows individuals to draw retirement allowance after only twenty years of employment which, for many workers, is years before their age makes it necessary for them to quit work.[313]

We must once again realize the value of strict and disciplined behavior—that diligence produces success and laxness engenders failure. A few slothful people can ride on the backs of a bustling society without becoming too burdensome or without slowing it down too much, but when the idle or underworking become large in number, society can no longer support itself. As demonstrated by the facts in Chapter I, American industry and technology are on the decline, our educational level continues to fall and poverty is more prevalent than ever in spite of billions of dollars spent on social programs.

### (i) Poverty

An American Civil Liberties Union Handbook for the poor, written to inform them of their rights and to encourage them to exercise those rights, states that poor people have the right to receive welfare, free medical care, food stamps, free or low-cost school lunches, public housing, legal services; go to court without paying court costs, day care and other services; and obtain unemployment compensation, tuition reductions or "scholarships" along with school breakfasts, and special food programs.[314] It is ironic that none of these "special rights of the poor" that the ACLU urges the poor to receive are employment or income-producing activities. Reduced tuition or scholarships are the only rights mentioned which have to do with constructive activity for the benefits received, and they will not result in gainful employment until several years of schooling are completed.

### (ii) Education

The cause of much of America's illiteracy is simply a lack of discipline and work on the part of the general population. Our teachers are often unable to write properly themselves. They have not mastered English, mathematics or other subjects they teach. Schools and parents do not demand their wards to work hard and learn. High rates of television-viewing from an early age make students passive in school and lazy at home.

As a result of government and judicial regulation, local school boards are often hampered in their attempts to remedy the problem. They are unable to dismiss incompetent teachers. Schools are unable to expel hostile and unruly pupils. School boards that attempt to enforce a dress code or instill ethics in education are often met with hostility by parents, judges and the media. Efforts to screen the books made available to students in the classroom are met with equal opposition by various counterproductive groups. Federal courts have even ruled unconstitutional school action prohibiting a male homosexual high school student from bringing a male date to a high school prom.[315]

Our institutions of learning must require a high standard of quality from the students if we are to train them to live in a technological world. For many years, educators had been advocating a progressive approach to education that did not require much discipline. For example, in order to be innovative and to make the principles of calculation enjoyable, educators of mathematics had done away with rote memorization and developed a "new math"[316] approach that proved to be as effective in teaching mathematics as alchemy is in teaching metalurgy. For twenty years, educators of English literature and the arts, trying to be creative, had been spreading theories that spelling and grammar rules inhibit a child's creativity. These educators claimed that children should be able to write as they please, so that they can express themselves.[317] This has proved to be nothing more than an excuse for sloppiness and has resulted in a generation of new teachers who are incompetent and incapable of proper instruction. We are beginning to realize our errors in this area but change is slow.

As for education, we must demand that discipline and hard work be once again a part of the school curricula. Education and all achievements come only through hard work and great effort. Our attempt to make learning painless has caused more pain in our youth than any straight-laced schoolmarm of our grandparents' era would ever mete out. That pain comes from a lack of learning and an absence of discipline. Hard work and learning can be painful until one adjusts and makes it a habit in life. Children must be taught principles of hard work in school or they will not be productive workers as adults. If our children learn proper habits and achieve a sense of accomplishment, then they will be prepared to enter society as productive citizens. Even if they do not learn many subjects in school, the principles of hard work will allow them to adjust to new situations. When confronted with a need for knowledge in a new area, they would have at their disposal the tools to learn it themselves. If our children do not learn these principles in school, they will be ill-prepared for work, and indeed, may never know the joys of honest endeavor. They may never learn how to achieve their full potential or even how to work at an acceptable level.

Progressive American philosophy asserts that true discipline comes only from full freedom of the individual to choose for himself whether to be disciplined or not. It claims that if discipline is pressed upon an individual, it is not discipline but a kind of forced labor which builds no lasting integrity.[318] In theory, this sounds like such a noble principle to enable the individual to choose for himself and singlehandedly rise above his base, undisciplined nature. In reality, however, it is nothing more than a ploy to eliminate unpleasant strictures enabling the formerly refined American to remain in his present feral state. Discipline cannot be acquired naturally any more than playing the violin can. Both require years of training to master, and until mastery is achieved, the individual cannot have a true choice of what to do with his life. Just as someone who is ignorant of music cannot pick up a violin and choose to play it at that time, the undisciplined cannot take up an activity and perform it in a disciplined manner. He has only two courses to pursue. He can remain unskilled in music, or discipline, or he can embark on a rigorous program to obtain the skill. Only at the end of that program, when mastery is achieved, can the individual truly have a choice between playing the violin, or being disciplined, on the one hand, and putting the violin aside, or abandoning discipline, on the other. Further, mastering a skill is much more difficult if started late in life so an individual must begin at an early age. The same applies to a youth who does not learn discipline as a child. He will have a much harder time acquiring discipline later because the rigorous training is too prohibitive. This is the status of much of America today; a people who lack discipline and effectively have not the choice to be otherwise.

### (iii) Industry and Technology

The causes of the dramatic decline in our industrial and economic growth and world industrial dominance which occurred in the 1970s are manifold. From 1949 to 1969, the output per man-hour of all persons employed in private business rose by more than 3 percent per year. In the 1970s that growth was cut in half and by the end of the decade productivity was actually declining.[319]

The various anti-growth movements, such as the consumer movement, the ecology movement, the hippie movement, the protect-the-wilderness movement, all opposed new developments, industrial innovation and increased use of natural resources.[320] In addition, government regulation of businesses and government expenditures on regulatory agencies increased dramatically. In 1970, the government spent less than $1 billion on regulatory agencies, by 1979, $5 billion.[321] During this same period, the number of government bureaucrats employed in regulatory agencies tripled, increasing from 28,000 in 1970 to 81,000 in 1979.[322] It took eighteen months to build the first nuclear power generator. It now takes twelve year. The $5 billion a year spent by the government for regulatory work is minor when compared with the costs to industry and the consumer of complying with federal government regulations. Conservative estimates put that cost in 1979 at approximately $100 billion per year.[323]

A major thesis of Nobel laureate economist Milton Freedman and other economists is that the benefits of federal government intervention into industry, at present, are offset by the extreme counterproductivity that results therefrom.[324]

Further, America's Christian work ethic has, in large part, gone the same way of Christianity. It no longer is as highly valued or is as important as it was in past eras. The concept that honest labor, independent of the remuneration accruing therefrom is, in and of itself, a worthwhile endeavor that is to be promoted by society is not as honored as it used to be. Administrative regulations, judicial mandates and goals of organized labor often work to undermine the promotion of honest industry. Unions rally in support of their own members when one is threatened with disciplinary action for misconduct, regardless of the individual's actual malfeasance. They generally do not take action to enforce a work ethic but only action to discourage working as a tool of collective bargaining. Judicial orders, threats of lawsuits and government regulation also act to discourage the employer from an effective promotion of work discipline.

The method to combat this erosion of our technological edge is to remove, to an extent, the federal regulatory and judicial control over industry.

# IV. SOLUTIONS AT LAW REGARDING STANDARDS OF CONDUCT

The solutions to the problems of the degeneration of our standards of conduct will not be easily achieved. The problems are complex; their causes are many and varied; and the people are not in concurrence with even the existence of the problems much less the methods of solution. These problems—divorce and the breakup of the home, unchastity, volume abortion, homosexual activities, a breakdown of our religious beliefs and code of morals, crime, drug abuse, the demoralization of our entertainment industry, widespread obscenity and pornography, excessive litigation, poverty, illiteracy, slowed technological growth, and decay of our public works and urban areas have been with us in varying forms and degrees since the dawn of civilization. However, in recent years the problems have become overwhelmingly large and deep-rooted in our society. We cannot claim to have improved even one of these problems since, say, the 1950s. Rates regarding crime, drug abuse, divorce, illiteracy and sexual permissiveness have all risen dramatically since then. We are certainly more technologically advanced than we were thirty years ago, but so is the entire world. The true measure of our technology is how we compare with the other nations. We have lost much of our competitive edge. Indeed, in key industrial areas, such as shipbuilding, steel production, automobile manufacturing and electronics, we have fallen drastically behind. In spite of Lyndon B. Johnson's and other presidents' "war on poverty," there are more poor who are more destitute than ever in our nation's history.

In order to solve these problems and arrest our decline, America must change many aspects of its society, in particular, its attitudes and actions. It must elevate its standards of conduct and once again make its code of morals a binding force in the community. America must construct its government so that it will be easy to do right and difficult to do wrong, and not the reverse. We must once again unify the nation behind a common system of beliefs and hard work with unity, not litigiousness. We must strengthen the family unit, encourage honest labor, reemphasize morality, chastity and discipline and deemphasize human sexuality. We must sternly prevent evil behavior and effectively educate our youth.

There is no clear-cut method to change our attitudes and actions to enable us to overcome our social ills. However, as mentioned earlier, we can return the structure of our laws to a form that will once again be conducive to right conduct. This would be accomplished by reempowering the states with the ability to govern and solve their own domestic problems.

Over time, the reach of our federal government has grown so long and powerful that it now covers almost every action of the people.[325] It is bulky and overbearing and often restrains effective measures to solve our problems,[326] whereas states, reempowered with the right to solve their problems could effect change on a local level and accomplish more efficiently the will of the people. This is the essence of the states' rights arguments that have existed since the Constitution was ratified in 1789. At this point an explanation of this argument is appropriate.

> The question of the relation which the State and General Government bear to each other is not one of recent origin. From the commencement of our system, it has divided public sentiment. Even in the convention, while the constitution was struggling into existence, there were two parties as to what this relation should be, whose different sentiments constituted no small impediment in forming that instrument. After the General Government went into operation, experience soon proved that the question had not terminated with the labors of the Convention. [327]

These words of John C. Calhoun, uttered on July 26, 1831, are just as relevant today as they were then, and the issue of federal-state relations is as pressing as it ever was. The U.S. Supreme Court stated in 1975 that: "Surely there can be no more fundamental constitutional question than that of the intention of the Framers of the Constitution as to how authority should be allocated between the National and State Governments."[328]

Despite this debate that continually rages over the extent of federal jurisdiction arising out of enumerated but undefined and indefinite powers, the Constitution of the United States is a truly remarkable document. Gladstone referred to it as "the most wonderful work ever struck off at a given time by the brain and purpose of man."[329]

The Constitution was fashioned by the representatives of "sovereign states" who had met for about a dozen years in a loose-knit confederation,[330] and who saw the need for a more powerful central government. Two cardinal features distinguish the republic created by the Constitution from all other political organizations in existence up to the time of its founding.

First, "in creating a new government the founding fathers sought to guard against the exercise of arbitrary power through a system of checks and balances referred to as the 'separation of powers' whereby governmental authority is divided between three branches of government to the end that each will serve as a limitation on the others."[331]

Second, "the framers resolved to further limit governmental authority by creating a dual or federal system, by delegating to a central government only those powers which conveniently could not be exercised locally while at the same time reserving to the several states the broad residuum of powers traditionally possessed by governments."[332]

The U.S. Supreme Court described this dual or federal system in *United States v. Cruikshank*[333] as follows:

> We have in our political system a government of the United States and a government of each of the several states. Each one of these governments is distinct from the other, and each has citizens of its own who owe it allegiance, and whose rights, within its jurisdiction, it must protect. The same person may be at the same time a citizen of the United States and a citizen of a State, but his rights of citizenship under one of these governments will be different from those he has under the other . . . .
>
> The government of the United States is one of delegated powers alone. Its authority is defined and limited by the Constitution. All powers not granted to it by that instrument are reserved to the States or the people. No rights can be acquired under the constitution or laws of the United States, except such as the government of the United States has the authority to grant or secure. All that cannot be granted or secured are left under the protection of the States.

Further, the U.S. Supreme Court stated in *Hammer v. Dagenhart*[334] that:

> In interpreting the Constitution it must never be forgotten that
> the nation is made up of States to which are entrusted the powers
> of local government. And to them and to the people powers not
> expressly delegated to the National Government are re-
> served . . . The power of the States to regulate their purely in-
> ternal affairs by such laws as seem wise to the local authority
> is inherent and has never been surrendered to the general govern-
> ment . . . . "

The central government's powers were vested in three branches: legislative, executive and judicial. Under the Constitution, the legislative power of the central government was to extend to 17 specifically enumerated subjects as well as to the enactment of "all Laws which shall be necessary and proper for carrying into Execution the foregoing Powers, and all other Powers vested by this Constitution in the Government of the United States or in any Department or Officer thereof."[335] The executive power was vested in a President whose functions were specifically to "take Care that the Laws be faithfully executed,"[336] to be the Commander in Chief of the Army and Navy, to conduct foreign affairs and other enumerated powers. The President was also to appoint, subject to senatorial confirmation, the federal judges and other officers of the United States not otherwise provided for in the Constitution.[337]

The judicial power was vested in a Supreme Court and other federal tribunals inferior to that Court which Congress might establish. The extent of federal judicial power was limited to cases and controversies based on either diversity of state citizenship or other factors concerning the persons or governmental units which were parties thereto, or of the character of the questions involved such as constitutional questions.

The powers of the federal government are vested in the three branches solely by virtue of the Constitution. The central government was one of delegated powers only. Moreover, the Founding Fathers felt that the exercise of these powers delegated by the federal government needed to be limited so that the rights of the citizens of the several states were protected. The Constitution was ratified only after assurances that limitations on actions by the federal government would be submitted by the first Congress in the form of amendments thereto. These limitations, known as the "bill of rights," were adopted three years after the ratification of the Constitution,[338] largely as a result of James Madison's insistence,[339] and are considered to be an integral part of the original federal system.[340] Under our dual or federal system any assertion of power by the federal government must be in accordance with the powers delegated to it by the Constitution. If the Constitution does not delegate the federal government the authority to act, then we need look no further; the federal government cannot act. If the Constitution does delegate power to the federal government in a certain area, then "we must go one step further and ascertain whether the mode in which that power is sought to be exercised transgresses any limitation contained in the bill of rights."[341]

Under the bill of rights, the federal government could do no act to restrain certain enumerated rights of the people even if it was acting under the color of certain delegated powers. Moreover, the tenth amendment provided "the powers not delegated to the United States by the Constitution, nor prohibited by it to the states, are reserved to the states respectively, or to the people."[342] In essence, this language merely set forth in writing an already existing principle and did nothing more than state the facts that the federal government's powers are delegated ones and not plenary. If the states, as independent sovereignties, did not delegate powers to the central government by the Constitution, then they retained those powers. By no other means does the federal government attain power but through delegation of the states. The states' rights debate centers on just how much authority should be vested in the central government and how much should be retained by the states and by the people. Advocates of centralization of governmental power accuse the states' rights advocates of being confederates and rebels,[343] racists,[344] and "radical in the extreme."[345] Advocates of a centralized government have traditionally looked to the government as a "mother figure" to solve most national ills, and, until the most recent trend away from big government, had been effective in attaining a centralization of power.

The development of centralization of power has been a gradual process which accelerated over the last twenty years. Originally, this centralization was feared by the Founding Fathers. Thomas Jefferson wrote to Joseph C. Cabell in 1816:

> What has destroyed the liberty and the rights of man in every government which has ever existed under the sun? The generalizing and concentrating of all cares and powers into one body, no matter whether of the autocrats of Russia or France, or of the aristocrats of a Venetian Senate.[346]

When our state was born, its founders saw government as a necessary evil. Their view was that the more government was "necessary," the more "evil" or oppression would result. As James Jackson Kilpatrick stated:

> It is inherent in the nature of man, whose first impulse is to act; it is inherent in the nature of the state, whose first duty is to restrain . . . The great men who long ago preceded us in this inquiry comprehended this conflict, this tension, with perfect clarity. They did not view the central government, as it is the custom to view it in the United States today, as a firm but loving *pater familias*, or in a less elegant image, as a comfortable sow with a hundred million teats.[347]

Thereinabove lies the states' rights debate. Centralization and big government on the one hand and division of power and local control on the other. A return to local control will be the vehicle for the American people to effect the change necessary to alter our current course toward ruin. In recent years, we expanded and extended the scope and authority of the central government to such an extent that the continued existence of our federal republic is in jeopardy. "One well may ask whether the states have not been reduced *vis-a-vis* the federal government, to well below the status of counties in the ordinary commonwealth. All this has been accomplished without the aid of constitutional amendment. If it stands, have we not replaced our Federal Republic with a unitary policy without even half trying to do so?"[348]

Long before Justice Rehnquist concluded in *Fry v. United States*[359] that "the Constitution was [not] intended to permit the result reached today; have we not driven another nail in the coffin of the Federal Republic?," officials representing many states met together in Biloxi, Mississippi, on July 27, 1962, and "speaking through the powerful Council of State Governments,"[351] addressed the issue of extension of Federal powers and concluded, as follows:[352]

"The characteristic of our constitutional government, which has contributed most to the development of democratic processes and the preservation of human rights is the division of the powers of government between the nation and the states on the one hand and between the executive, legislative and judicial departments of both state and federal governments on the other. Over the years we have escaped the evils of despotism and totalitarianism. It is only when each division of the whole governmental structure insists upon the right to exercise its powers, unrestrained by any other division, that the proper balance can be maintained and constitutional government, as we understand it, preserved.

"It is the responsibility of the central government to protect the people from invasion by the states of those rights which are guaranteed to them by the Federal Constitution. It is equally the obligation of the states to initiate and to prosecute to fruition the necessary procedures to protect the states and the people from unwarranted assumption of power by any department of the federal government.

"The most sacred duty of all public officials, whether state or federal, and the highest patriotic responsibility of all citizens is to preserve, protect and defend the Constitution, including that portion of the Constitution intended to guarantee a government of dual sovereignty. When it becomes apparent that purposely or inadvertently any department or agency of government has embarked upon a course calculated to destroy the balance of power essential to our system, it behooves all other departments and agencies acting within their respective spheres of jurisdiction to take all steps within their power necessary to avert the impending evil. We believe that grave imbalance now exists.

"Some federal judicial decisions involving powers of the federal and state governments carry a strong bias on the federal side, and consequently are bringing about a strong shift toward the extension of federal powers and the restraint of state powers. This shift tends to accelerate as each decision forms the basis and starting point for another extension of federal domination.

"A greater degree of restraint on the part of the United States Supreme Court can do much, but experience shows that it is not likely to be sufficient. The basic difficulty is that the Supreme Court's decisions concerning the balance between federal and state power are final and can be changed in practice only if the states can muster sufficient interest in Congress, backed by a three-fourths majority of the states themselves to amend the Constitution. While the founding fathers fully expected and wished the words of the Constitution to have this degree of finality, it is impossible to believe that they envisaged such potency for the pronouncements of nine judges appointed by the President and confirmed by the Senate. The Supreme Court is, after all, an organ of the federal government. It is one of the three branches of the national government, and in conflicts over federal and state power, the Court is necessarily an agency of one of the parties in interest. As such, its decisions should not be assigned the same finality as the words of the Constitution itself. There is need for an easier method of setting such decisions straight when they are unsound.

"To amend the Federal Constitution to correct specific decisions of the federal courts on specific points is desirable, but it will not necessarily stop the continuing drift toward more complete federal domination. The present situation has taken a long time to develop and may take a long time to remedy.

Accordingly, some more fundamental and far-reaching change in the Federal Constitution is necessary to preserve and protect the states.

"We appeal most earnestly to all branches of the federal government, and particularly to the highest federal court, to take diligent and impartial reflection upon the dangers to the nation inherent in the trends herein described. We urge them to evaluate the possibilities of an all-powerful central government with unlimited control over the lives of the people, the very opposite of self government under a federal system.

"It is the ultimate of political ingenuity to achieve a vigorous federal system in which dynamic states combine with a responsible central government for the good of the people."

Basically, the power of the federal government just grew over time, little by little, through a judicial activism which characterized the Warren and Burger courts, but was prevalent in other courts as well. The meaning of judicial activism is attempting to achieve social reform through judicial decision. Judge Jerome Frank described this process by saying that "judges work back from conclusions to principles."[353] A more detailed explanation of judicial activism is as follows: Judges formulate out of the record and the arguments a tentative conclusion as to what justice and the law require. Then the judge searches for theories and authorities to support the tentative conclusion.[354] Judges excuse this approach claiming, "it is psychologically impossible even to approximate objectivity and impartiality."[355]

The two major constitutional theories by which the activist courts have extended their power to control state activities are the commerce power and the fourteenth amendment. Concerning the commerce clause, legal scholars have stated: "During the forty years since the New Deal, social control has inexorably consolidated in the expanding federal bureaucracy on the strength of the commerce power and the spending power,"[356] and "during the Depression years, the country suffered the spectacle of the court distorting the Commerce clause completely out of proportions so as to drastically expand federal power."[357]

Concerning the fourteenth amendment, legal scholars have pointed out: "The ironical fact of all this is that the so-called enlightened 'liberal' who today invokes the [fourteenth] Amendment for his own selfish aims invariably professes to be conducting some divinely inspired crusade, yet nothing in the history of this country is more immoral, fraudulent or high-handed than the manner in which the Fourteenth Amendment was adopted."[358]

It is not the purpose of this author to trace the tortuous precedents concerning the commerce clause and the fourteenth amendment which have empowered the federal govenment to control the affairs regulated by the states.

Nevertheless, as for the fourteenth amendment, a brief history of the development and interpretation is in order, due to the recommendations this author makes concerning it.

The history of the "ratification" of the fourteenth amendment which provides in part "that no state shall deprive any person of life, liberty, or property, without the due process of law," is as follows:[359]

> The Fourteenth Amendment was submitted by a Congress dominated by a radical republican leadership which never would have suceeded had Lincoln lived.
>
> The Constitution requires a two-thirds vote of both houses to submit an amendment for ratification. While the submission was by two-thirds of those present, this two-thirds was obtained only by excluding, under reconstruction acts, representatives of ten Confederate states, notwithstanding the fact that the Constitution also provides that each state shall have at least one representative in the House. If the Southern delegation in Congress today were to forcibly eject representatives of other states and seek to submit a repeal of the amendment, would anyone seriously contend their actions legal?
>
> Consequently, it follows that the Fourteenth Amendment was never legally submitted.
>
> However, even passing by the illegal submission, it is equally clear that the amendment was never legally ratified. Adoption under the Constitution required ratification by at least three-fourths, or 28, of the 37 states then in existence.
>
> Kentucky, Delaware and Maryland rejected the amendment outright. The amendment has never been ratified by California. New Jersey and Ohio initially ratified it but both later withdrew their ratification. All ten of the Southern states immediately rejected it. The Amendment failed.
>
> Assuming for the moment that the submission was legal, this rejection was lawful and proper under the procedure provided by the Constitution. That should have been the end of the matter. But Congress became infuriated, and thenceforth adopted high-handed measures.
>
> It enacted, over President Johnson's veto, the Reconstruction Act of 1867, which declared that no legal government existed in the ten states, placed them all under military occupation, disfranchised the white people, and put the state governments

in the hands of illiterate Negroes, scallawags and carpet-baggers. In another section, this wholesale bill of attainder provided that each excluded state must ratify the amendment in order to enjoy the status of a state, including representation in Congress. It was only under such duress that the amendment was finally adopted.

As mentioned earlier, the bill of rights originally applied only to the federal government. The states ratified the Constitution on the promise that further restraints on enumerated federal power would be adopted by means of a bill of rights, and this was done. The Constitution contains an enumeration of powers expressly granted by the states to the federal government. This indicated that the Constitution is an enabling and not a restraining instrument.[360] By virtue of this fact, since the states did not restrict themselves in the bill of rights, the various state legislatures were free to act on the rights contained in the first ten amendments as they saw fit, subject to approval by the state supreme court review and not the U.S. Supreme Court.

Accordingly, states could pass laws outlawing what they perceive to be obscenity and pornography, fornication, adultery, homosexual acts, abortion, and other social ills. They could empower their school boards with the right to dismiss incompetent teachers without fear of civil rights reprisals. States could impose the death penalty, crowd the jails and deny the prisoners recreation facilities without fear of federal courts ruling that such acts were unconstitutional. In sum, any right contained in the bill of rights could be handled in a manner the state governments saw fit.

The adoption of the fourteenth amendment provided the U.S. Supreme Court with the opportunity to change that. Through a series of cases, the U.S. Supreme Court construed the due process clause of the fourteenth amendment (which was applicable to the states) in a manner which made the bill of rights also applicable to the states. At that point, the U.S. Supreme Court empowered itself to review all action by the states in regard to bill of rights issues and pass on their constitutionality.

Historically, "due process" meant that the federal government would not deprive someone of his rights without following lawful procedures. This meant that in order to send a suspect to jail there had to be a duly conducted trial held first. This concept is embodied in numerous laws and ordinances besides the Constitution. The concept of due process was expanded by dividing it into two areas, one called procedural due process, the traditional concept, and one called substantive due process. Procedural due process concerned the legal procedure employed to deprive an individual of his rights.

The procedural due process safeguards ensured that the individual charged with a crime would be assured of the right to such things as:
- -notice of the nature and cause of the charge against him;
- -a speedy and public trial by an impartial jury;
- -opportunity to confront witnesses accusing him and to compel witnesses in his favor to appear;

Furthermore, the individual would not be:
- -subjected to unreasonable searches or baseless arrests by government officials;
- -compelled to incriminate himself.

These and other procedural rights are incorporated into the bill of rights. The concept of substantive due process was developed to extend the power of the court's authority beyond the mere enforcement of proper procedure when depriving a person of life, liberty or property, to include the power of the court to guarantee what it saw as a basic liberty. At this point it no longer was sufficient for Congress or the states to pass laws which restrict the actions of the citizens. Even if they did so according to proper, established procedure, i.e. due process of law. Every act of Congress or the states which could affect an implied constitutional right became subject to judicial scrutiny. The courts would determine if a right is guaranteed under the Constitution by implication, and if it was, the court could rule it unconstitutional in the event the court thought it unjust. Hence, the courts, for example, were able to read into the Constitution the guarantees of the right of a woman to have an abortion, even if elected legislators enacted laws to make it illegal. Under other amendments contained in the bill of rights made applicable to the states by the fourteenth amendment, the U.S. Supreme Court has been able to invalidate state anti-pornography statutes, state penal codes, zoning laws, etc.

The result has been that in recent years the power and the rights of the communities and citizens of the various states to promote programs and use their duly enacted laws to maintain their traditional value system has been curtailed by the U.S. Supreme Court and other federal courts as well. Once the U.S. Supreme Court granted itself jurisdiction over state action, it began to cast aside various state action governing standards of conduct as being unconstitutional. At times it would find an entire state statute to be unconstitutional and at other times only portions thereof. Because of this social activism on the part of the U.S. Supreme Court, states in the 1960s began to raise questions about the Court's present-day function. At the meeting in Biloxi, Mississippi, of the Council of State Governments in 1962, this issue was the major topic of debate. Many states were saying that the U.S. Supreme Court, comprised of unelected officials, was legislating laws rather than merely interpreting them.

State legislatures, striving to maintain order and strong communities, have traditionally dealt with various moral issues by enacting laws which they felt were intrinsic to a wholesome society. However, at present, the U.S. Supreme Court and other federal courts have removed from the state legislatures their rights and powers to legislate freely in these areas, deciding that communities did not have the right to self government on these fundamental issues but that the U.S. Supreme Court would have final say thereon. States began to say the U.S. Supreme Court had indeed become what Thomas Jefferson feared—an oligarchy of despots. They now legislate the laws of the nation rather than merely interpret them and have thereby taken the right of self-determination away from the people.

As it stands now, there is no purpose in maintaining separate state constitutions or state laws. On vital social issues, the federal courts have removed the power to which the states were originally entitled to construct and construe their own laws. Regarding less vital issues, over which the federal courts grant power to the states to enact legislation, the result is a lack of uniformity contributing to the needless growth of lawyers to interpret them. Why should there be fifty different versions of the Uniform Commercial Code or bedding tagging laws and only one version on school prayer? States should be allowed the freedom to determine their own laws on these fundamental issues. Such constitutes a federal system and is the way that the American system was originally structured. For most of this country's history, states have had adequate power to govern themselves. However, recent trends toward centralization of power have severely curtailed these states' rights.

States' rights movements call for an interpretation of the Constitution which would limit the powers of the dual government to assume implied powers (as opposed to express ones) and give meaning to the tenth amendment requirements of reserved powers of the states. This doctrine of states' rights does not mean state sovereignty, which would constitute a rejection of the principle of national supremacy under the Constitution: "Lest the advocates of the tenth amendment be misunderstood, they are not asking that New Hampshire join the United Nations or that Georgia have an embassy in Warsaw. In things 'national', the Article I, Section 8 powers of the national government are gladly recognized. But to confuse our constitutional means with ends and to ignore the purpose of that great document will deny our people the right to much longer enjoy the blessings of liberty."[361]

When we talk of limiting the powers of the federal government we are concerned only with implied powers thereof. There is no debate as to the express powers of the federal government. These are many and are fundamental to a united nation. However, the U.S. Supreme Court, other federal courts and even Congress with increasing fervor in recent years, have been enlarging the role of the federal government by taking a concept in the Constitution and expanding it to include vaguely related principles, giving rise to so-called implied federal rights. For example, Article I, Section 8 of the Constitution provides that Congress shall have power "to regulate commerce with foreign nations, and among the several States, and with the Indian Tribes." Congress and the federal courts reasoned that race relations affect commerce and since Congress may regulate that area, it may regulate race relations to the exclusion of the states. Accordingly, the power to regulate racial discrimination was delegated to the federal government by implication and the U.S. Supreme Court approved. Thus there was no violation of the tenth amendment guarantee of states' rights.

The interpretation of the fourteenth amendment by the U.S. Supreme Court has altered our federal system. The U.S. Supreme Court, by its own social activism, has assumed legislative control over the states and now decides issues of race relations, religion, abortion and many other pivotal issues which determine whether or not a society progresses or regresses. The U.S. Supreme Court thus makes decisions that no state or community can alter no matter how wrong the decisions are and no matter if 100 percent of the population votes to have them altered.

In spite of all we do as individuals to elevate the morality of the nation, our efforts will be thwarted by the strictures of unconstitutionality placed upon the legislatures by the federal courts. Courts, in their attempt to restrict the states from depriving individuals of freedom, have, in fact, deprived the community of its rights and have mandated the legislation of immorality, and the abandonment of our entire heritage. Even though these court-formulated strictures would themselves be unconstitutional under normal interpretations of the tenth amendment and other provisions of the Constitution which empower the federal government with rights, there exists no body to correct the injustice. These strictures have been placed on the states by the U.S. Supreme Court which has final say as to the constitutionality of a law or ruling, so unless it recognizes its own acts of usurpation and voluntarily relinquishes its powers to Congress and the states, we are, with the exception of one procedure, powerless to force the courts to comply with the Constitution. This means that communities will not be able to legislate or take action to halt their moral decline, but must abide by a national standard set by a nine-person board on every fundamental issue in existence. Everything that a community prizes highly is subject to being cast aside at the mere whim and discretion of a majority of said board who are proven to be social activists by nature and tradition. Never in the history of America has so small a group had so much power, and they are wielding it to our destruction.

There exists a solution. It is simple, direct and imminently possible to achieve through action at the local level. Direct national action would not even be necessary to once again return the constitutional rights of the states and the people to their elected representative bodies. All that would be required would be uniform state action. Local legislatures could enact measures to force the courts to return to them their lawful rights to draft legislation as they deem prudent.

This action would be accomplished by repealing the fourteenth amendment to the Constitution and strengthening the tenth amendment guarantees of states' rights. Since the federal courts use the due process clause of the fourteenth amendment to gain supervisory power over the the states on key issues, the repeal of this amendment would effectively remove the court-created basis on which federal judges rely to regulate state action so extensively. To repeal the fourteenth amendment would be to eliminate the due process clause applicable to the states, with which the U.S. Supreme Court and the federal government have appropriated the constitutional rights of the states. This would mean that only the various state supreme courts and not the U.S. Supreme Court could pass on the constitutionality of these key issues, and they would do this based on the U.S. Constitution and the respective state constitutions. Due process, as applied to the federal system would still exist in the fifth amendment and in federal statutes such as the Federal Rules of Civil Procedure, etc., and due process would exist for the states as set forth in their constitutions and other laws and statutes. The basic rights of the citizens, as they concern the government's obligation to abide by the laws in its disposition of life, liberty and property, will be unaffected. What will be altered is the power the U.S. Supreme Court has assumed to invalidate state action on issues that are so fundamental to a community's wholesome development. The supremacy of the Constitution and the federal govenment would remain unchallenged. Our country would still be centrally controlled in areas of national interest, taxation, military, international affairs, commerce, and other areas expressly delegated to the federal government by the U.S.Constitution. Only the issues of local concern, standards of conduct and racial identity would be affected thereby.

Many eminent legal scholars advocate the removal of U.S. Supreme Court jurisdiction over states' rights issues. Jesse H. Choper, Professor of Law, University of California, Berkeley states:

> Federalism has been a central element of the American polity from the nation's inception to the present day. Many of the most salient provisions of the Constitution and its amendments concern the distribution of governmental authority between the nation and its component states . . . .[362]
>
> The major thesis of . . . the Federalism Proposal, may be stated briefly: the federal judiciary should not decide constitutional questions respecting the ultimate power of the national government vis-a-vis the states; the constitutional issue whether federal action is beyond the authority of the central government and thus violates "states' rights" should be treated as nonjusticiable, with final resolution left to the political branches.[363]

Whether or not the U.S. Supreme Court abandons judicial review of federalism questions, or whether or not states' rights prevail or a strong centralized government prevails is not, of itself, the most important issue. The states' sovereignty is not the primary entity which must be maintained at all costs. Instead, society's primary concern ought to be for the people as a whole and the maintenance of a political system that encourages proper conduct and discourages antisocial behavior. A state is but an artificial entity, the product of a man's brain and a means to an end. It is a device to permit people to live together in peace and contentment.[364]

A strengthening of states' rights by repealing the fourteenth amendment is merely a device to remove an unwieldly federal government's undue restrictions from the people to enable them to enact laws that elevate our standards of conduct. If Congress and the U.S. Supreme Court had not taken the rights of the individual to such an extreme to the detriment of society as a whole, the states' rights debate could be one exclusively for historians and legal scholars. As it is, it is an issue of crucial importance. Local legislation is the means whereby the nation can once again enact laws that make it easy to do right and difficult to do wrong, thereby helping to avert America's decline.

There is no guarantee that all states will enact legislation to promote good principles. Some states, for example, may take swift action to encourage discipline in our schools and with our bodies; others may not. But at least the choice will be up to the people and not up to a five-person vote of a nine-person Supreme Court.

E. Freeman Leverett convincingly sums up the reasons for states' rights as follows:[365]

When we speak endearingly today of state's rights, there immediately arises the inclination to assume that the recipient of our homage thus bestowed is the state as a political entity itself.

But such is not the case. State's Rights must be held inviolate, not because of any belief in the state *per se*—in the context of freedom all governments are suspect; but rather it is because that through the division and limitation of powers inherent in the federal system, the rights of the individual can be best preserved against the evils of concentrated, centralized power which history discloses has forever presaged the destruction of liberty.

It may be that wars may desecrate our cities and lay waste the countryside, but we can gain strength from assurances that they can be restored in time;

It may be that the tempestuous forces of nature will play havoc with our agriculture and render barren the fields of grain; but the enlightened, progressive determination of rugged individualism will in time bless us with our former station; It may be, that foreign powers through intrigue or otherwise may sweep our commerce from the seas, but we can be confident another virile generation will in time renew it;

But if the magnificient edifice of constitutional government is lost, there shall have passed from this earth never to rise again, the most sublime, the most profound and the most precious system of government ever fashioned by human hands.

The method to preserve this nation is set forth more fully later in this text.

# V. ANALYSIS OF PHILOSOPHIES WHICH FOSTER OUR DECLINE —PART TWO

## 1. Introduction

In Chapter III we examined the philosophies behind the degeneration of America's standards of conduct and the effect thereof on our behavior. In the previous chapter we examined and recommended a course of action for rejuvenating these standards through amending the Constitution to enable states to once again have power over their own laws. In this chapter we will examine the causes and effects of our philosophies on our identity and future as a people.

In recent years, those whom the world traditionally recognizes as Americans[366] (those of Western European stock) have been taught to disregard the richness of their heritage and identity and even be ashamed of it. In certain circles of our society, it is deemed to be misplaced pride to value the achievements of our ancestors and our race. To pride oneself on being descended from the Founding Fathers is often considered to be hollow boasting. Yet, our forefathers founded this nation and drafted the Constitution for their posterity and for no one else's,[367] so, in fact, those that can, should rejoice in being of their lineage and heir to that birthright. Recent commentators often write more pages falsely characterizing our ancestors as being wicked, poor, motley, greedy and oppressive than they write praising them for their accomplishments and virtues.[368] America must value its past and rejoice in its rich heritage, or forever lose that heritage to other races who value theirs.

There is a direct link between our past and our future. If we despise, make light of, or ignore our past, we cannot pass on our identity and culture to our posterity. Our children will abandon our culture and the ideals we hold.[369] They will increasingly marry into other races and allow those races to continue immigrating to America *en masse* until America is no longer white but thoroughly mixed. At that point, national unity will become impossible to regain until we are unified as one dark-skinned race. This darkening of America is rapidly taking place today, and we are so confused by our identity that no one can speak out against it and feel comfortable in society. Unless we remember our heritage and strive to preserve it for our posterity, America will be overrun and ruined.

In today's society, the topic of racial classification is itself a confusing and sensitive issue. It is confusing because many people feel that the ideal posture to assume in this regard is to ignore all differences between peoples and count individuals of every race as one's kith and countrymen if they merely reside within the political boundaries of one's country.[370] It is sensitive because much of our society feels that references to race (particularly those made by whites) generally result from an underlying sense of racism or bigotry.[371] Moreover, our society has undertaken a comprehensive campaign to attempt unification and integration of all peoples into one harmonious body, outlawing the public from segregating or discriminating on the basis of race in such areas as housing,[372] education,[373] employment[374] and miscegenation.[375] Any person making statements viewed as undermining the campaign is subject to being labeled racist or possessing racist sentiment.[376] For example, if a white man were to say, "I want to work, live and associate only with people of my own race, just as my parents did before me and as most of the world does now," he would be accused by much of our society as being a white supremist and a bigot, regardless of his true regard for other peoples.[377] In order to avoid the ugly designation of white supremist and bigot, the average American strives to ignore differences between the races and live a life in an ever-darkening America.

Because racial classification is such a sensitive issue, disinterested study and discussion on related topics is often impossible. Anthropology is one of the least exact of all sciences in its usage of terms, classifications and groupings. Anthropologists have generally classified man into three primary groups: Caucasoid, Negroid and Mongoloid.[378] These classifications are based upon color of skin and eyes, facial and bodliy proportions and form of hair but are inadequate to classify the various races of man,[379] particularly in modern America where so many different peoples presently reside. Because of the inadequacy of these three anthropological groupings and due to a failure on the part of the anthropologist to supply more specific groupings, the general puplic, including the government, has employed its own unscientific terms to fill this need, based primarily on appearance (such as "white" and "black"), origin (such as "Asian" and "Samoan") or culture (such as "Latin").[380]

In the practical world, the term "Caucasoid" is particularly inadequate in classifying races. The Caucasian race, so named from the erroneous notion that the original homes of the hypothetical Indo-Europeans was the Caucasus Mountains,[381] designates peoples from Europe, North Africa, the Near East and India. The Caucasian race is loosely called the "white race" but it includes many darker-skinned peoples.[382] According to the anthropological groupings, a Hindustani and a Dane are classified as being of the same race even though their differences are literally like night and day.[383] For purposes of governmental statistics, both English and Lybians are classified as whites.[384]

This lack of adequate classification often results in diverse groups such as Mexicans and Iranians being indistinguishable for statistical purposes from Northern Europeans, which further adds to the confusion and lack of precision in this area. Moreover, because of the extreme sensitivity surrounding the issue of racial classification, many people think that this confusion and inadequacy of terms is a positive development.[385] They assert that classification in itself is evil.[386]

## 2. Outline of Incorrect Philosophies on Racial Identity

As mentioned above, we often do not prize our heritage, culture, religion, posterity and unity as a people. As a result, we allow other races and peoples to immigrate and reproduce in large numbers and ultimately replace us as Americans. In short, the large influx of other races into America is the outside force that is the direct cause of our impending ruin. The indirect causes are the incorrect philosophies we have adopted that allow this direct cause to have effect. The incorrect philosophies regarding our identity will be discussed in this part of the text. Further, this part will deal with the issue of race, how America is being replaced with other peoples and how our incorrect philosophies regarding identity allow this to happen.

Some incorrect notions subscribed to by a large number of Americans and which prevent us from preserving our nation are as follows:

1. Maintaining the racial composition of a society is racist.
2. America is a country for all races. Except for the American Indians from whom we took this land, all Americans are immigrants, so to restrict immigration or citizenship to whites only is unAmerican.
3. History has proved that our past racial discrimination was groundless. Racial diversity enhances our influence in the world community and gives us vitality that racially homogenous countries do not have.

4. It does not matter if Americans become a nonwhite people.

Following is an analysis of the abovementioned notions.

1. Maintaining the racial composition of a society is racist.

The International Convention on the Elimination of All Forms of Racial Discrimination provides that "racial segregation . . . [is] condemned by the States' parties, and they pledge to prevent, prohibit and eradicate all such practices in their territories."[387] This UN-sponsored convention is express in its position that maintaining racial identity and communities of one's own people is racist. Further, articles in the UNESCO Courier assert that "integration, both racial and cultural, is certainly an indispensable step on the road to the eradication of racialism."[388]

In our society, the word "racism" is the most powerful tool of the liberal elements to defeat action to maintain our racial composition. Articles in law reviews and other magazines proclaim: "Racism is a disease that defies easy remedy."[389] "Racism: The world [*sic*, word] is charged with a certain ugly vitality."[390] "Racists Are Made, Not Born."[391]

In order to determine if preserving one's people and heritage is an act of racism, it is necessary to analyze that concept. "Racism" is "the assumption that psycholcultural traits and capacities are determined by biological race and that races differ decisively from one another which is usually coupled with a belief in the inherent superiority of a particular race and its right to domination over others."[392] Others state that racism has three component parts: i) that there are pure races; ii) that these pure races are biologically superior; and iii) that this superiority explains and justifies their predominance and privileges.[393]

Let us examine each of these components in light of a community's desire to maintain its racial composition.

i) There are pure races.

Liberal publications on the subject of race state that geneticists generally concur that there is no such thing as a "pure race"[394] and man's present biological nature developed, and is still developing, in the course of continuous cross-breeding processes. They state: "In this context, therefore, the concept of purity is no more than a metaphor, wishful thinking, fantasy."[395] The foregoing statement may be true, but it is immaterial to America's communities. It does not matter whether there are pure races, particularly to the American who wants to live only among his own people.

Certain amounts of cross-breeding may have indeed occurred in the course of human development. However, limited mobility in past ages minimized its extent and effect. With the exception of the New World, particularly parts of South America, rarely in the history of mankind has cross-breeding and integration taken place as is beginning to occur in this country. Brazil has seen heavy intermixing "where Iberians, Slavs, Anglo-Saxons and others have become inextricably mixed with black and Amerindian peoples and with Arabs, Jews and Japanese."[396] The result is often a dark people with strong Negroid features. Under conditions that exist today in America (limited white reproduction and immigration and very heavy nonwhite reproduction and immigration), the natural result will be a dark, Negroid/Oriental people similar to Brazil, but vastly different from our original heritage.

Whether the Western European race of our Founding Fathers is pure or not is immaterial. The fact is Americans, until this generation, were, on the whole, fair-skinned children of our forefathers and are now fast becoming colored aliens. Action to halt this could not constitute racism.

ii) These pure races are biologically superior.

Whether one race is inherently superior to another in certain areas has been a topic of debate for centuries,[397] with prevailing viewpoints and so-called "proof" changing with the political and social sentiments and the people. Traditionally, white Americans thought they were biologically superior to the nonwhite races.[398] As Professor A. Montagu of Princeton University pointed out, this feeling of superiority, in part, stemmed from the achievements of whites in relation to the darker races.[399] Then, with the advent of the civil rights movement, and before, the prevailing theories among geneticists, anthropologists, psychologists and other scholars shifted to the position that the mental and physical capacities of all races and ethnic groups are much the same.[400] Currently, there is a trend toward the erosion of the idea of equality in intelligence of races.[401] Trends are now in support of doctrines which indicate that heredity, genetics and race are inalterable factors in mental, physical and personality traits of man.[402]

Undoubtedly, the controversy will rage for many more years with the prevailing theories switching with the sentiments of the researchers and the people. However, whether the mental capabilities of one race are naturally superior and that of another are naturally dull, is, in large part, immaterial to the American who desires to maintain his cultural and racial identity. Whether whites are more intelligent than blacks or more caring than Orientals or whether the black, brown and yellow races of man are actually more honest or moral than the white race does not change the fact that a white America is becoming colored and new peoples are replacing the Americans in their own country.

Certain facts and statistics of Chapter I and other trends not discussed herein indicate that currently white America is failing on many fronts and that Orientals are succeeding at every endeavor. One might conclude that Orientals are superior to whites, but it does not follow that Americans should want their nation to become Oriental or should encourage Oriental immigration. Indeed, whites might feel even more concern at mass immigration of superior aliens because they will assume control of the nation sooner. In sum, the second test of racism, biological superiority of races, is inapplicable to the American wanting to preserve his country. Americans should want to retain control of their country from other races and peoples regardless of their genetic makeup.

iii) Superiority explains and justifies their predominance and privileges.

Superiority and inferiority, as a factor, is irrelevant to the case for maintaining one's country. The view that traditional concepts of racial and cultural identity and purity are racist and are sociological overgrowth from a more barbaric era is incorrect. Pride in one's heritage and race is not racism. In reality, racial and cultural unity is an extension of the most basic unit of civilization—the family and the community. By trying to uproot America's Western European heritage and society and replace it with a mixture of peoples, we only act to tear down the unity and harmony of a people. Hence, through an exercise of reasoning and seeming intelligence, we are orchestrating the breakdown of many of our ideals and beliefs that have made America great and are thus destroying ourselves as we try to progress. Maintaining the racial compositon of a society is not racist.

2. America is a country for all races. Except for the Indians, from whom we took the land, all Americans are immigrants. Thus, to restrict immigration or citizenship to whites only is un-American.

Contained in the above statement are several incorrect beliefs which prevent America from taking action to preserve our nation for our people. They are discussed below.

i) We took the land from the Indians.

At the time of Columbus, it is estimated that there were as few as eight million Indians in all of North and South America.[403] How could we have taken 16,424,000 square miles[404] from eight million people? The fact is America was a vast, untamed wilderness waiting for Americans to cultivate it.

ii) America is a country for all races.

As we saw in Chapter I, until the 1950s, America was ninety percent white.[405] The remainder were primarily Negroes. Negroes did not come here in large numbers. The total number of Negroes brought over to America was roughly 350,000.[406] The rest of the immigrants have primarily come in this generation.

iii) To restrict immigration or citizenship to whites only is un-American.

The history of immigration law in America discredits the belief that to restrict immigration or citizenship to whites only is un-American. For most of the nation's history, immigration was severely restricted by race. The first American nationality law, enacted by Congress on March 26, 1790, restricted eligibility for naturalization to "free white persons."[407] This designation of "free white persons" as the sole group eligible for naturalization continued unchanged for eighty years, until the end of the Civil War.[408]

In 1857, the U.S. Supreme Court in *Dred Scott v. Sanford* said that "they [Negroes] had no rights which the white man was bound to respect, and...the negro might justly and lawfully be reduced to slavery for his benefit. He was bought and sold, and treated as an ordinary article of merchandise and traffic."[409] In sum, the U.S. Supreme Court declared that "Negroes were never intended to be citizens,"[410] and thereby "forever" barred them from the rights of citizenship.

The ultimate result of this decision was the Civil War. The emancipation of Negroes thereby and the control of the U.S. Congress by radical Republicans during the reconstruction era resulted in relaxation of the naturalization restrictions against them. And the Act of July 14, 1870, directed that "the naturalization laws are hereby extended to aliens of African nativity and to persons of African descent."[411]

The naturalization of Chinese was specifically prohibited in the Chinese Exclusion Act of May 6, 1882,[412] and was not repealed until the 1940s.[413]

In the 1920s, the U.S. Supreme Court held that because Japanese were not white, they could not be citizens of the U.S.[414] Later, a Hindu claiming to be white sought admission to American citizenship. In refusing his application, the Court said:

> It may be true that the blond Scandinavian and the brown Hindu have a common ancestor in the dim reaches of antiquity, but

the average man knows perfectly well that there are unmistakable and profound differences between them today.[415]

From the 1920s through the 1940s, Afghans,[416] Persians[417] and Arabs[418] had been declared ineligible for citizenship. In short, for most of this nation's history, immigration and citizenship were limited to white persons only.[419]

3. History has proved that our past racial discrimination was groundless. Racial diversity enhances our influence in the world community and gives us vitality that racially homogenous countries do not have.

Recent articles and polls indicate that most Americans feel that racial diversity enhances our world influence while foreign countries feel that diversity hinders it. Foreigners have explained it in this manner: "White Americans have built up a considerable amount of goodwill in the world through their upright dealings. That goodwill is being eroded by the change in racial makeup of the nation. No one knows how a colored America will act in world economics and politics. The entire world has looked to America to be the arbiter of their disputes and problems. They regard the white man as the neutral party and the natural leader to help them solve their problems. As America becomes increasingly nonwhite, the degree of trust the rest of the world places in America's leadership ability dramatically decreases."[420]

We lose our effectiveness as leaders when no one relies on us or can trust us because of our nonwhite and fractionalized nature. Rather than giving us vitality, racial diversity has given us strife and conflict and is enormously counterproductive. Indeed, the issue of race has caused more conflict, misery and death than any other issue in the United States. Abraham Lincoln stated to a large Negro delegation in Washington D.C.:

> See our present condition— the country engaged in war, our white men cutting one another's throats, then consider what we know to be the truth. But for your race among us there would be no war.[421]

Ever since the poem written by the Jewess, Emma Lazarus, was inscribed on the Statue of Liberty in 1903, Americans have had it ingrained in them that their shores are to be the final destination of the world's unwanted. That poem, familiar to most, reads as follows:

> Give me your tired, your poor,
> Your huddled masses yearning to breathe free.
> Send these, the hopeless, tempest-tossed to me,

I lift my lamp beside the golden door!

We have somehow come to believe that our strength is derived from the illiterate masses of the third world rather than through a systematic growth of a unified country accepting hardworking additions only from the same source from which America sprang—Europe. This relatively new concept, "the Statue of Liberty syndrome," has distorted our view of our country's strengths and weaknesses. Our nation was strong and unified before the word "melting pot" was used at the beginning of this century to describe certain cities in America, and it remained strong throughout the delicate era of heavy immigration during this period because the waves of immigrants from Europe could easily assimilate themselves into America's European heritage. The only substantial barrier that the Poles, the Scandinavians or Germans had to overcome was the English language. Once they learned English, they were able to become full, well-adjusted citizens of the country. "The children of English, French, German, Italian, Scandinavian, and other European parentage quickly merge into the mass of our population and lose the distinctive hallmarks of their European origin."[422] Their old-country customs were not dissimilar from America's customs which had been derived basically from England, the Netherlands, France, etc. Their religion (Christianity) was the same, only the sects were sometimes different, and even then the only real difference between Catholicism, the religion of many of the new immigrants, and Episcopalianism or Presbyterianism was that the Catholics had a stronger affiliation to Rome, rather than to London or Edinburgh. The Mormons, an indigenous American sect of Christianity that sprung up in the 1830s amid New England Protestant revivalism and comprised of Protestants, had a harder time fitting into their own American culture than did any immigrant from the various Catholic countries.

Those afflicted with the Statue of Liberty syndrome seem to always use the Irish experience as an example and say: "Look at them; they were discouraged from coming to America and discriminated upon arrival, but they have adjusted. The reasons for discrimination against the Irish were groundless, just as groundless as discrimination is against the nonwhite immigrants of today." It seems that people often point out discrimination against the Irish Catholics to show how wrong discrimination is and how all peoples should be welcomed to America. The Irish experience of the last century does not compare with the nonwhite immigration of today. First of all, there could never be a more American lot than the Irish Catholic immigrants of the late 1800s and early 1900s. They were from the British Isles, spoke English, had the same culture and the same family names as the Americans who had been in this country for two centuries before them. The attempt to separate them from the rest of America is an attempt to further fractionalize the country and keep it in disunity.

Discrimination against the Irish was relatively mild and was based on two factors. First, territorial fears that a great number of immigrants would divide the nation and cause the Americans to lose their land and possessions. Second, the historical, but intense animosity between the Protestants and the Catholics of the British Isles. The Americans feared that the same problems would erupt here, which has proved not to have occurred. America was able to absorb the large number of Irish immigrants because their differences were minor and would vanish in one generation. The same can be said for the immigrants from the other European countries. Such is not the case with the Iranians, Laotians, Samoans or Puerto Ricans. It is more than just silly to say that because the Germans and the Irish adjusted so can the nonwhites; it is fatal to the future of our country. Nonwhite presence in America will continue to rive the country and prevent progress until we fall apart or are totally overrun. America cannot harbor the world's refugees, particularly when the entire nonwhite world desires that classification with the ultimate aim of becoming American. To make America a white country again is consistent with our history. No nation on earth can point a finger at us or even think ill of us for protecting our borders. They all do it with their own laws and occasionally by force. The world will only wonder why we waited so long.

4. It does not matter if Americans become a nonwhite people.

Judge Walter B. Jones of Alabama stated in 1957:[423]

Truly a massive campaign of super-brainwashing propaganda is now being directed against the white race, particularly by those who envy its glory and greatness. Because our people have pride of race we are denounced as bigoted, prejudiced, racial propagandists and hate-mongers by those who wish an impure, mixed breed that would destroy the white race by mongrelization. The integrationists and mongrelizers do not deceive any person of common sense with their pious talk of wanting only equal rights and opportunities for other races. Their real and final goal is intermarriage and mongrelization of the American people.

I do not know whether or not the above statement is true. Was there a "massive campaign of super-brainwashing propaganda" being undertaken at that time? I do know, however, that much of America now feels that intermixing is acceptable, that open disapproval thereof is evil and that there is no purpose in maintaining our white identity in America.

Such an attitude is the ultimate treachery to our society. An individual who advocates, or tolerates, the nation becoming nonwhite is, in fact, an anarchist, either actively or passively, who would allow everything our forefathers established to be destroyed. There is no more deadly or destructive act of treason than this, and it must be combatted.

The attitude of today that we are proud that the America of tomorrow will be a nonwhite one is an attitude which defies understanding and explanation except to someone who has lived through the relentless attacks on our white heritage occurring these last twenty years. If any other country in the world were being inundated by aliens as America is, civil war would have broken out and the invaders repelled. No country would condemn them. We, however, feel constrained to do nothing and thus we are giving away our country. If we were living in a different age, the situation with which America is now struggling—the swelling numbers of nonwhites—would be called an invasion. The President would have declared war and the press would incite the citizenry to unite to meet the foe with the valor and determination due the most righteous of causes. The legislative branch of the government would introduce a flurry of emergency measures designed to throw the ominous power that this country possesses behind the noble cause of a just war. The people would rally; patriotism, love of country and sense of duty would sweep the nation. America would meet the foe and subdue it. In a past age, the American people would have overcome this gravest of threats and returned to their homes victorious. We do not, however, live in such an age.

## 3. General Thoughts in Summation

Indeed, the most marked difference between America of 1956 and America of 1986 is the change of the racial composition of the people and the effect that this has had on the entire country. No longer are we a country of one people united behind a common European heritage and sects of a common religion. Many of our communities are no longer comprised of our distant relations or children of our fathers' friends. Our neighbors often come from radically diverse backgrouds and dissimilarities are often greater than similarities. Every community is affected. Even communities that are still wholly white are profoundly affected by the consequences of racial and cultural diversity. The governmental policies, laws and regulations which affect all citizens are heavily influenced by our diverse racial makeup. Our educational policies, our industry, our national identity, our entertainment, newspapers and magazines, our music and our morality are all affected by these recent changes in our nation's race, religion, culture and heritage.

Our country was generally unified and constituted one or maybe two peoples until the recent change in our racial makeup. In many ways we are now a fragmented people, made up of every race and hue conceivable. We must move toward unification again; we must become one people, one race and one culture in order to maintain a democracy and a United States. However, as the number of immigrants swell, as white Americans bear and rear fewer children and as the whites and nonwhites increasingly intermarry, the ultimate result may be an actual unification of peoples and cultures, but Americans will no longer be of the same race or culture as their founding fathers. In other words, as the trends indicate, the America and Americans of yesterday will not be the ones of tomorrow. The land will still exist with people still living on it and the people may even call themselves Americans and abide by permutations of our Constitution, but they will not be Americans as we and our fathers conceived them to be. There will be no link between the past and the future. In short, America will not exist and so has no future. The signs of, and acts by, a people with no future are ever present in this "me-generation", "live-for-now" society of today.

As of October 1984, "minorities" are the majority in twenty-five big cities, including Los Angeles, Chicago, Detroit and San Antonio.[424] Our largest cities are no longer American. They used to be unified, safe and white. Now they are blights on our nation's reputation and burdens on the backs of America. The inner cities are among the most hostile and dangerous places on earth.

The result is that America's heritage is being overthrown and the country is being invaded and destroyed. The American people are engineering their own collapse. Never before in the history of the world has a people voluntarily relinquished their country to invaders. Never before has a country enacted laws to turn its lands and government into the hands of aliens. The laws are such that they encourage the flood of alien "minorities" and social taboos frustrate any legitimate attempt to preserve or reclaim our country.

In a sense, we are a nation of self-haters who deny our heritage and past. We do not stand up and support the cause of the white for those who do are labeled and are despised by their fellow countrymen. Not so with the other races in America. They may forcefully and stridently demand anything they desire and are noted for standing up for their so-called rights. Blacks can cast their votes for Jesse Jackson for President for reasons of race alone and they may, and do, publicly encourage that.[425]

It is time for the American people to speak out and demand that we retain our identity. Americans have the right to be unified into one nation and one people under a common system of beliefs and values and a common heritage and racial identity.

# VI. THE AMENDMENT

## 1. The Scope of the Amendment

The one, effective way to maintain a strong, unified America that can be inherited by our posterity is to return to the definition of citizen that was *de facto* through the 1950s and *de jure* until 1868. Up to the 1950s and beyond, the only real and full citizens, in fact, were the whites. Although nonwhites had gained nominal citizenship rights before that time, the Jim Crow laws prevented them from exercising those rights.[426] Prior to 1868, nonwhites could not even be citizens due to the U.S. Supreme Court ruling in the *Dred Scott*[427] decision which the fourteenth amendment overturned. In essence, this section of the text advocates a return to the *Dred Scott* ruling and submits a proposal for repealing the fourteenth amendment which would make that event a reality.

This proposal has been drafted with two objectives in mind. The first one is practicablity in making the proposal law and the second one is achieving a fair and non-burdensome adjustment as the status and situation of the nonwhite population. We have already discussed above how a repeal of the fourteenth amendment would reenable states and communities to effectively grapple, on a local level, with their problems regarding standards of conduct. It has been shown that a repeal of the fourteenth amendment would allow states and communities to take certain remedial measures on local issues affecting standards of conduct regardless of recent decisions of the U.S. Supreme Court. As mentioned above, it has been asserted that the U.S. Supreme Court has enabled itself to supervise state action through interpretation of the fourteenth amendment's due process clause made applicable to the states. The U.S. Supreme Court has relied on this clause to infer federal power to regulate state action. Thus, the U.S. Supreme Court and federal courts have given themselves power to strike down duly enacted state and/or local statutes dealing with capital punishment[428] and terms of imprisonment[429], abortion[430], prayer in schools[431], nativity scenes[432], sexual and homosexual regulations[433], obscenity and pornography[434], disposition of illegal aliens[435], racial issues[436] and many others, all in the name of due process under the fourteenth amendment to the Constitution.

A Chief Justice of the U.S. Supreme Court once declared, "The Constitution is what judges say it is."[437] That should not be true, but, sadly, it is. By fiat, the U.S. Supreme Court has dislodged and abandoned the concept of political freedom and has put in its place a doctrine of judicial activism. As early as 1958, the state supreme courts recognized that the U.S. Supreme Court was acting with an increasing lack of judicial self-restraint and concern for prior established decisions in the field. "This was pointed out most dramatically by the Conference of Chief Justices (a conference of the chief justices of the state supreme courts) in 1958 in its 'Report of the Committee on Federal-State Relationships as Affected by Judicial Decisions.' The report was unique in that it was a formal criticism, with documentation of cited cases, of the United States Supreme Court by the state supreme court chief justices. They formally indicted the Supreme Court for lack of judicial self-restraint and predicted a mounting crisis unless the federal judiciary returned to the time-honored concepts of judicial interpretation in keeping with the fundamental philosophy on which this republic was founded. The 14th Biennial General Assembly of the States, held in Chicago in December, 1958, commended the chief justices' report."[438]

Since that indictment, the situation has worsened and judicial activism and control over national affairs has exceeded all fears of the Founding Fathers when they established our governmental system of checks and balances. If the fourteenth amendment were repealed, the U.S. Supreme Court would no longer be able to rely on the due process clause to empower itself with manufactured rights of review and legislation. That review would be left to the state supreme courts and legislation would be returned to the elected bodies.

In addition to having the above effect, the repeal of the fourteenth amendment would assist in returning the citizenship status of nonwhites to that of the *Dred Scott* era, that is, nonwhites would again become non-citizens.

The fourteenth amendment is quoted below in full to enable the reader to understand its contents and the rationale for rescission thereof.[439]

## ARTICLE XIV

*Passed by Congress June 16, 1866. Ratified July 23, 1868.*

Section 1. All persons born or naturalized in the United States, and subject to the jurisdiction thereof, are citizens of the United States and of the states wherein they reside. No state shall make or enforce any law which shall abridge the privileges or immunities of citizens of the United States; nor shall any state deprive any person of life, liberty, or property, without due process of law; nor deny to any person within its jurisdiction the equal protection of the laws.

Section 2. Representatives shall be apportioned among the several States according to their respective numbers, counting the whole number of persons in each State, excluding Indians not taxed. But when the right to vote at any election for the choice of electors for President and Vice President of the United States, representatives in Congress, the executive and judicial officers of a State, or the members of the legislature thereof, is denied to any of the male inhabitants of such State, being twenty-one years of age, and citizens of the United States, or in any way abridged, except for participation in rebellion, or other crime, the basis of representation therein shall be reduced in the proportion which the number of such male citizens shall bear to the whole number of male citizens twenty-one years of age in such State.

Section 3. No person shall be a senator or representative in Congress, or elector of President and Vice President, or hold any office, civil or military, under the United States, or under any State, who having previously taken an oath, as a member of Congress, or as an officer of the United States, or as a member of any State legislature, or as an executive or judicial officer of any State, to support the Constitution of the United States, shall have engaged in insurrection or rebellion against the same, or given aid or comfort to the enemies thereof. But Congress may by a vote of two thirds of each House, remove such disability.

Section 4. The validity of the public debt of the United States, authorized by law, including debts incurred for payment of pensions and bounties for services in suppressing insurrection or rebellion, shall not be questioned. But neither the United States nor any State shall assume or pay any debt or obligation incurred in aid of insurrection or rebellion against the United States, or any claim for the loss or emancipation of any slave; but all such debts, obligations, and claims shall be held illegal and void.

Section 5. The Congress shall have power to enforce, by appropriate legislation, the provisions of this article.

It should be noted that Section 1 is the only important section of the entire amendment. The Section 2 language as to apportionment of representatives is found in Article I of the Constitution and the rest of Section 2 and the remaining sections contain nothing but punishments directed against the southern States for seceding from the Union.

The fourteenth amendment is an amendment that reflected the zeal of the day and should be repealed. Basically, it grew out of the Northerners' desire to humiliate the South and exact revenge from them for rebellion. It should not be maintained at the expense of the nation as a whole. Of all the laws contemplated by the Congress and the state legislatures, the most important legislation for the preservation of our union would be the proper repeal of this amendment.

There have been many efforts over the years to repeal the fourteenth and fifteenth amendments and to have them declared invalid. Below is a Senate Resolution of the Georgia General Assembly which sought to do just that. It explains in a clear manner the historical argument that the amendments are invalid.[440].

*Senate Resolution No. 39 (Res. Act No. 45) of the 1957 regular session of the Georgia General Assembly, passed March 8, 1957, memorializes the United States Congress to declare the Fourteenth and Fifteenth Amendments to the United States Constitution invalid. The resolution follows:*

### RESOLUTION ACT 45

"A memorial to the Congress of the United States of America urging them to enact such legislation as they may deem fit to declare that the 14th and 15th Amendments to the Constitution of the United States were never validly adopted and that they are null and void and of no effect.

"*Whereas*, the State of Georgia together with the ten other Southern States declared to have been lately in rebellion against the United States, following the termination of hostilities in 1865, met all the conditions laid down by the President of the United States, in the exercise of his Constitutional powers to recognize the governments of states, domestic as well as foreign, for the resumption of practical relations with the Government of the United States, and at the direction of the President did elect Senators and Representatives to the 39th Congress of the United States, as a State and States in proper Constitutional relation to the United States; and

"*Whereas*, when the duly elected Senators and Representatives appeared in the Capitol of the United States to take their seat at the time for the opening of the 39th Congress, and again at the times for the openings of the 40th and the 41st Congresses, hostile majorities in both Houses refused to admit them to their seats in manifest violation of Articles I and V of the United States Constitution; and

"*Whereas*, the said Congresses, not being constituted of Senators and Representatives from each State as required by the Supreme Law of the Land, were not, in Constitutional contemplation, anything more than private assemblages unlawfully attempting to exercise the Legislative Power of the United States; and

"*Whereas*, the so-called 39th Congress, which proposed to the Legislatures of the several States an amendment to the Constitution of the United States, known as the 14th Amendment, and the so-called 40th Congress, which proposed an amendment known as the 15th Amendment, were without lawful power to propose any amendment whatsoever to the Constitution; and

"*Whereas*, two-thirds of the Members of the House of Representatives and of the Senate, as they should have been constituted, failed to vote for the submission of these amendments and

"*Whereas*, all proceedings subsequently flowing from these invalid proposals, purporting to establish the so-called 14th and 15th Amendments as valid parts of the Constitution, were null and void and of no effect from the beginning; and

"*Whereas*, furthermore, when these invalid proposals were rejected by the General Assembly of the State of Georgia and twelve other Southern States, as well as of sundry Northern States, the so-called 39th and 40th Congresses, in flagrant disregard of the United States Constitution, by the use of military force, dissolved the duly recognized State Governments in Georgia and nine of the other Southern States and set up military occupation or puppet state governments, which compliantly ratified the invalid proposals, thereby making (at the point of the bayonet) a mockery of Section 4, Article IV of the Constitution, guaranteeing 'to every State in this Union a Republican Form of Government,' and guaranteeing protection to 'each of them against invasion;' and

"*Whereas*, further, the pretended ratification of the so-called 14th and 15th Amendments by Georgia and other States whose sovereign powers had been unlawfully seized by force of arms against the peace and dignity of the people of those States, were necessary to give color to the claim of the so-called 40th and 41st Congresses that these so-called amendments had been ratified by three-fourths of the States; and

"*Whereas*, it is a well-established principle of law that the mere lapse of time does not confirm by common acquiescence an invalidly-enacted provision of law just as it does not repeal by general desuetude a provision validly enacted; and

"*Whereas*, the continued recognition of the 14th and 15th Amendments as valid parts of the Constitution of the United States is incompatible with the present day position of the United States as the World's champion of Constitutional governments resting upon the consent of the people given through their lawful representatives;

"*Now, therefore, be it resolved by the General Assembly of the State of Georgia:*

"The Congress of the United States is hereby memorialized and respectfully urged to declare that the excusions of the Southern Senators and Representatives from the 39th, 40th, and 41st Congresses were malignant acts of arbitrary power and rendered those Congresses invalidly constituted; that the forms of law with which those invalid Congresses attempted to clothe the submission of the 14th and 15th Amendments and to clothe the subsequent acts to compel unwilling States to ratify these invalidly proposed amendments, imparted no validity to these acts and amendments; and that the so-called 14th and 15th Amendments to the Constitution of the United States are null and void and of no effect.

"*Be it further resolved* that copies of this memorial be transmitted forthwith by the Clerk of the House and the Secretary of the Senate of the State of Georgia to the President of the United States, the Chief Justice of the United States, the President of the Senate and the Speaker of the House of Representatives of Congress of the United States, and the Senators and Representatives in the Congress from the State of Georgia."

Repeal of the fourteenth amendment and thereby reinstating the *Dred Scott v. Stanford* ruling that nonwhites cannot be citizens is a proper and necessary action for the preservation of the American people. Absent such legal safeguards for the American people, the course of modern America will continue until we are completely replaced by a new race of people.

The method for achieving this repeal, resulting in the revesting of the states with their rights to cure domestic problems regarding standards of conduct, and the unification of the American people and retention of our racial identity, would be through the ratification of the following amendment to the Constitution, to be numbered the twenty-seventh amendment.

## ARTICLE OF AMENDMENT XXVII

Section 1.

The fourteenth and fifteenth articles of amendment to the Constitution of the United States are hereby repealed. Further, in order to halt the encroachment into the reserved powers of the states by the United States and its judicial branch, the tenth article of amendment is hereby amended to read as follows:

> The powers not expressly delegated to the United States by the Constitution, nor prohibited by it to the States, are reserved to the States respectively, or to the people.

Section 2.

No person shall be a citizen of the United States unless he is a non-Hispanic white of the European race, in whom there is no ascertainable trace of Negro blood, nor more than one-eighth Mongolian, Asian, Asia Minor, Middle Eastern, Semitic, Near Eastern, American Indian, Malay or other non-European or nonwhite blood, provided that Hispanic whites, defined as anyone with an Hispanic ancestor, may be citizens if, in addition to meeting the aforesaid ascertainable trace and percentage tests, they are, in appearance, indistinguishable from Americans whose ancestral home is the British Isles or Northwestern Europe. Only citizens shall have the right and privilege to reside permanently in the United States.

Section 3.

The Congress and the several states, except where expressly preempted by the Congress, shall have concurrent power to enforce the provisions of this article by appropriate legislation, in coordination with the President, as such legislation concerns the making of treaties pursuant to Article 2, Section 2 of the Constitution.

Section 4.

This article shall be inoperative unless it shall have been ratified as an amendment to the Constitution by the Legislatures of three-fourths of the several states within seven years of its submission.

## 2. Analysis of the Sections

The following is a section by section discussion of the suggested twenty-seventh amendment.

## (a) Section 1.

Section 1 of the amendment would repeal the fourteenth as well as the fifteenth amendments and would amend the tenth amendment by inserting the word "expressly" before the word "delegated." The fourteenth amendment has been quoted above. The fifteenth amendment is quoted below.[441]

### ARTICLE OF AMENDMENT XV (1870)

Section 1.

The rights of citizens of the United States to vote shall not be denied or abridged by the United States or by any State on account of race, color, or previous condition of servitude.

Section 2.

The Congress shall have power to enforce this article by appropriate legislation.

A repeal of the fourteenth and fifteenth amendments will have two basic effects. It will eliminate the absorption doctrine whereby the U.S. Supreme Court has expanded the bill of rights protections to cover state action and, thus, ultimately usurp states' authority.[442] Lest there be any doubt in the minds of the U.S. Supreme Court justices, the tenth amendment is amended as well to ensure this result. It will also terminate the right of citizenship by virtue of being born in the United States and could return the law to the state it was in after the *Dred Scott* decision. Since the fourteenth amendment directly reversed that decision, a repeal of the fourteenth amendment could terminate that reversal. The fourteenth and fifteenth amendments are the only references in the entire Constitution which can be interpreted to bestow the rights of citizenship on nonwhites. In order to ensure this result, Section 2 of the suggested amendment is included. This issue will be discussed in detail in the analysis of Section 2 below.

Much discussion has heretofore been given on the states' rights issue and how a reempowering of the states with their reserved powers will enable our country to reestablish our standards of conduct. Therefore, further discussion on this point need not be given. It is appropriate, however, to recite the following from the South Carolina Act of February 14, 1956, Calendar No. S.514 which is one of many state resolutions in recent years advocating a reempowering of the states with their reserved powers. It should be noted that this Act was submitted to Congress and the President of the United States by then State Senate President, Ernest F. Hollings, who ran for president in the Democratic primary of 1984.[443]

> The genius of the American Constitution lies in two provisions. It establishes a clear division between the powers delegated by the States to the central government and the powers reserved to the States, or to the people. As a prerequisite to any lawful redistribution of these powers, it establishes as a part of the process for its amendment the requirement of approval by the States.
>
> The division of these powers is reaffirmed in the Tenth Amendment to the Constitution in these words: "The powers not delegated to the United States by the Constitution, nor prohibited by it to the States, are reserved to the States respectively, or to the people."
>
>      *          *          *
>
> [T]he action of the Supreme Court of the United States constitutes a deliberate, palpable, and dangerous attempt to change the true intent and meaning of the Constitution. It is in derogation of the power of Congress to propose, and that of the States to approve, constitutional changes. It thereby establishes a judicial precedent, if allowed to stand, for the ultimate destruction of constitutional government.

A repeal of the fourteenth amendment will do much to terminate the illegal encroachment by the central government into the reserved powers of the States and the rights of the people. However, a repeal of that amendment alone might not be sufficient in light of the extremely activist nature of the U.S. Supreme Court. The U.S. Supreme Court has impliedly bestowed powers on itself and the other branches of the central government in blatant disregard for the tenth amendment. A mere repeal of the fourteenth amendment may eliminate the due process theory on which the courts have relied to assume ultimate control over the people but might not prevent them from reaching the same ends by different means. The repeal of the fourteenth amendment is but a treatment of the symptoms, not a cure of the disease. The cure is a reinforcement of the tenth amendment.

The Texas Legislature recognized this fact and by House Concurrent Resolution proposed as follows:[444]

> House Concurrent Resolution No. 5 of the second 1957 special session of the Texas Legislature proposes that a national convention be called, as provided by Article V of the United States

Constitution, to amend the constitution so as "to clearly and specifically set out certain limits beyond which the United States government has no authority, as generally provided in the Tenth Amendment. . ."

## HOUSE CONCURRENT RESOLUTION NO. 5

WHEREAS, The Constitution of the United States is based upon the principle of proper limits being placed on the exercise of all power by all governments and officials, both state and national; and

WHEREAS, The people of the United States have historically believed in a written constitution rather than rule by proclamation; and

WHEREAS, The exercise of power by the United States Government has become so great and centralized as a result of the United States Supreme Court's liberal interpretation of the powers ascribed to the United States Government under the United States Constitution so as to threaten the very existence of all State Governments and states' rights except as political subdivisions of the United States; and

WHEREAS, The United States Supreme Court has virtually repealed the Tenth Amendment by interpretation which has resulted in a central government almost without limit of its powers; and . . . .

WHEREAS, The Texas Legislature further feels that individual rights and freedoms are best protected by limiting the powersof government rather than centralizing them; and

WHEREAS, The Legislature of the State of Texas recognizes that the easiest way for a foreign enemy to control the United States is to centralize all power and control in one central government rather than have all powers divided and limited among an "indivisible union of indestructible states"; and

WHEREAS, Article V of the United States Constitution provides a method whereby two thirds of the States' Legislatures can petition Congress for a National Convention to propose an amendment to the United States Constitution to clearly and specifically set out certain limits beyond which the United States Government has no authority, as generally provided in the Tenth

Amendment . . . .

As set forth above, the Texas legislature petitioned Congress and the President to amend the Constitution so as to reinforce the meaning of the tenth amendment. The suggested amendment accomplishes this purpose by inserting the word "expressly" to further limit the powers of the federal government. When the proposed tenth amendment was discussed at the first Congress, the word "expressly" was suggested as a clarification of the limitation on the power of the federal government.[445] The Hamiltonians, or Federalists, rejected this proposal while the Madisonians, or states rights advocates, supported it.[446] The Hamiltonians won, and the word did not become a part of the tenth amendment. However, if the Hamiltonians could have seen how meaningless the tenth amendment would become, surely they would have not opposed the insertion of the word.

### (b) Sections 2 and 3.

The citizenship clause of fourteenth amendment is no longer practical in today's mobile society where foreigners come to live in the United States for a few years with their families. Children are born in the United States and, by virtue of the citizenship clause of the fourteenth amendment, these children become American citizens, when, in reality, they have no more of a nexus with this country than a birth certificate. Pregnant Mexicans, Filipinos and other minority women abuse this clause to gain citizenship for their children by sneaking into this country to have their babies.

Often is the case where a Japanese or Korean company will send a young family to the United States and a baby is born here. When the family returns to its native country, the parents reenter their own country with their Japanese or Korean passports and the baby has a separate U.S. passport. The baby, with no more ties to the Unites States than a birth certificate, becomes a citizen entitled to live here with the foreign family it brings with it on its next visit. As for the Mexican families who come to America, their companies do not send them, nor do they have proper visas. They come into the country by themselves, illegally, but their children still become citizens. The whole world is taking advantage of these ridiculous laws that allow our country to be turned over to non-Americans. The amendment to the Constitution that this text proposes would plug that one loophole which makes children of Americans and children of illegal aliens equally American under the law. The sheer force of numbers necessitates this change. There are only 200 million actual Americans, but under current laws, there are 4 billion potential ones.

Further, as mentioned above, we are seeing not just a massive influx of minorities into the country, but are witnessing an epidemic of miscegenation within the native population, which in the space of two generations will darken and alter the racial composition of our entire nation. Opponents of the suggested Amendment question the right of society to take such drastic action against the minorities and the American whites who want to marry them. The answer is simply that the right develops partly out of necessity. If action is not taken, white America is a doomed race. It is the illegal aliens, the pressing mass of minorities and the misceginators who have no right to unalterably destroy the race, heritage, culture and entire makeup of our nation.

The repeal of the fifteenth amendment fits into the overall scheme of the proposal of this text by removing the right to vote regardless of race. It would be incongruous to repeal the fourteenth amendment which gives citizenship rights to nonwhites, but not repeal the fifteenth amendment which gives them voting rights. Moreover, as stated above, in the Georgia Senate Resolution, the fifteenth amendment as well as the fourteenth amendment was illegally proposed and ratified by the radicals at the end of the Civil War.

This step of repealing the fifteenth amendment ultimately is necessary because as the hoards of what we now call minorities increase, they will soon have a more powerful franchise than the so-called American majority. At that juncture, what had been mainstream America will not be able to pass one law. We will then be at the mercy of a nonwhite majority who will, and are now, no matter how much we try to deny it, act, and are acting, to curtail our freedoms. Soon America could be like the former Rhodesia where power is turned over to the nonwhites and the whites are forced to flee for their protection. Then America could be like a large Haiti, the once white population gone, its once thriving economy collapsed, and its system of democracy having long since passed away.

Repealing the fourteenth and fifteenth amendments would be the first step to ensure an America for Americans. However, repealing these two amendments alone could possibly have no effect at all on the current situation. The fourteenth amendment was enacted to void the *Dred Scott* decision, which held that blacks were not citizens, and the fifteenth amendment was enacted to give the blacks the right to vote. However, the mere repealing of these amendments would not necessarily mean that the *Dred Scott* decision would govern the land. It could mean only that all explicit references granting nonwhites rights of citizenship would be deleted from the Constitution. The U.S. Supreme Court has rendered many decisions since *Dred Scott* which have construed the citizenship rights of nonwhites. Moreover, legislatures have enacted many civil rights bills. The court decisions and the bills of Congress were all based upon these new rights granted by the fourteenth and fifteenth amendments, and there is logic in the argument that when one removes a foundation, all things that are built theron must fall. Nevertheless, the final arbiter of this issue would be the U.S. Supreme Court itself. In its reasoning, it would likely conclude that the repeal of the fourteenth and fifteenth amendments merely removes express language granting citizenship rights to nonwhites. The Court could find that implied rights still exist. It could overrule *Dred Scott* and provide nonwhites with citizenship based upon implied rights. It could let all previous legislation and U.S. Supreme Court decisions stand on these implied rights rather than express ones. The end result would be that the ultimate decision of America's future would be up to a majority of a single group of nine justices.

Accordingly, it is necessary to use positive wording in the proposed amendment rather than merely deleting past additions. Such positive wording is set forth in Section 2 of the suggested twenty-seventh amendment. The wording, clearly stated, may cause an immediate negative reaction in Americans who have been so intensely conditioned to think that any distinction in race is evil. Probably the most common reaction will be that of disbelief that such an amendment could even be considered. Before this reaction overwhelms the reader, I would like to examine the reasons behind those reactions. From experience, I know that Japanese, Chinese, Mexicans or Africans would not react in this manner. Their laws and their practices act to maintain their country for themselves. The reason for our negative reactions is, as mentioned above, our conditioning. The memory of Hitler's racism, for example, conjures up repulsive images which condition us. The end result is we have become unable to distinguish between policies to maintain cultural and racial identity and policies to destroy large sections of humanity. This lack of discernment is a major cause of our ruin. Basically, nonwhites have this discernment. By and large, they understand that this country is really the property of the whites, and they know that they would do the same, were their country threatened with being taken from them through immigration. Therefore, because the ones already in this country are aware of their tenuous title to citizenship, they may protest all the louder to further condition Americans to think the ideas of a unified, white America (the views of our grandparents) are evil.

As mentioned in the previous chapter, much in our society acts to condition us to reject our heritage, and as the nonwhite forces grow stronger, the pressure and conditioning will intensify until remedial action will be no longer possible. At this stage, action is possible if all of us shake off the years of conditioning that have dulled our perception and look at this proposal with a clear, rational mind, weighing the facts, the trends and ultimate justice (justice not construed to be what is easy or nice to each individual who may appear oppressed, but justice that can be disciplined and even harsh when needed). We must look to the future and envision what the results of inaction will be.

Section 2 of the draft twenty-seventh amendment is divided into two parts. The first one defines what a citizen of the United States is. The second part states that only citizens shall have the right to live permanently in the United States. Section 2 will return the definition of U.S. citizen to its traditionally accepted form.

There is nothing new in the concepts presented herein. Wherever there lives a nation which prizes its national identity and entrenches its future existence behind political boundaries, there the fundamental principles expressed herein are accepted and applied. The struggle of nations, races, religions and cultures to retain their separate identities is common politics all the world over. That, in its essence, has been the philosophy of peoples. So, the underlying principle of this amendment is the simple doctrine of nationalism.

### (i) Definition of White

In order to enforce this amendment as it relates to the vast majority of people, there is no real need to define the term "white of the European race". This is because most Americans can be easily defined as either white or nonwhite. Someone of English, German, Swedish or Polish ancestry would never be confused as being nonwhite. Conversely, a Negro, a Chinese, an Arab, and most Mexicans are, by appearance, obviously nonwhite. The division between whites and nonwhites can easily be drawn in the vast majority of cases. There are, however, arguments and complexities concerning a small percentage of the people which can be carried to the extreme to bog down the entire process of defining who should and who should not be a citizen of the United States. Moreover, since America is now preoccupied with the concepts of individual rights over the rights of the country as a whole, this issue of unclear lines between white and nonwhite can deter some people from supporting the amendment. With each year the problem becomes more and more complex.

Such problems concern the classification of part-white/part-nonwhite peoples, or nonwhite Caucasoids such as those from Iran, Armenia, and other parts of Asia, etc. For example, many states had laws providing that a person with one-eighth or one-fourth African, American Indian, or Asian blood was classified as nonwhite[447]. Opponents to such classifications have asserted that the same logic should be applied in reverse, that is, someone who is one-eighth European should be classified as white. In this manner, much of the black community could claim to be white due to past racial mixing, giving rise to confusion and frustration of progress. The end result of this would be that the Americans will have rationalized away their country. The point to be made here is that this delicate issue of classification can be used to thwart any attempt to solve America's racial problem. Accordingly, we must artfully draw a line and maintain it. We should not let small problems obscure the large picture.

As mentioned above, in the recent past, America had clear standards to determine who was white and who was nonwhite; who would be eligible for citizenship and who would not. We must readopt those measures and classifications or calamity will result. If America would only resort to the citizenship requirements of as recently as the 1940s and 1950s, our heritage would not be in such jeopardy. We could, with slight modification, return to those laws to effect a proper solution to our racial problems. Certainly a reversion to that principle will not be simple, but it is necessary and can be accomplished with a minimum amount of difficulty.

The language used to define who will be a citizen is taken from various instances in American law. Until recently, in a number of instances in the United States, classifications based on race, color, ancestry or national origin have been utilized for the purpose of drawing distinctions in legal rights and obligations[448]. "Statutory definitions of race [were] generally based on the individual's blood, ancestry, appearance or a combination of these factors. Moreover, the factor of blood is further subdivided into the so-called proportion or percentage test and the ascertainable trace test. The statutes may provide that a person is a member of the racial group either if he has a stated per cent of the blood of that group in his veins or if he has any ascertainable trace of the blood of that group. Definitions which utilize ancestry as the basic factor generally provide that a person will be deemed a member of the racial group affected if he has an ancestor who was a member of that group within a specified number of generations removed."[449]

Section 2 adapts a combination of these three tests, ascertainable trace of blood, ancestry and appearance. For the Negro, the test is any ascertainable trace. For the other nonwhites, the test is more than one-eighth or more than one great-grandparent who is nonwhite, and for Hispanics, it is appearance and distinguishability from other Americans in addition to the ancestry test.

Separate tests for Negroes and other nonwhites had been the law in a number of jurisdictions when such laws were commonly on the books. Virginia's code, for example, employed the ascertainable trace test for Negroes and an ancestry test for American Indians.[450] Mississippi's miscegenation statute, a typical example, proscribed marriage between a white person and a Negro "or persons who shall have one-eighth or more Negro blood or with a Mongolian or a person who shall have one-eighth or more Mongolian blood."[451]

The distinction between the tests for Negroes and other nonwhites results partially from the fact that so many of the laws of various jurisdictions considered persons with even slight Negro admixture as being Negro, and partially because, as Lincoln put it: "You and we [blacks and whites] are different races. We have between us broader differences than exists between almost any other two races."[452] Courts have held that persons of as little as one thirty-second Negro blood were Negro and thus excluded from attending a white school.[453]

The test in the suggested amendment for other nonwhites such as Mongolians or American Indians is less strict than some statutes, such as the Mississippi miscegenation statute cited above which requires persons to be less than one-eighth Mongolian to be classified as white (in the proposed twenty-seventh amendment, a person of one-eighth Mongolian blood would be a white, but under the Mississippi code, he would not have been) and the Virginia Code of the 1950s which requires the person to have one-sixteenth or less of American Indian blood, and no other non-Caucasian blood to be deemed to be white.[454] Section 2 is, however, as strict and at times more strict than some statutes that define race.[455] A one-eighth test is used for nonwhites who have no Negro blood because it is perceived that this percentage is small enough for the person to appear to be white and assimilate into the American community. Moreover, there will be very few individuals in this category around whom debate as to their ancestry would arise. There are indeed very few non-Negro, non-Hispanic persons with one-eighth or less nonwhite blood who do not appear to be entirely white.

Under section two of the suggested amendment, Hispanics are subject to both the one-eighth test and the appearance test. This is a result of the magnitude of the recent Hispanic immigration into this country and the mass confusion as to their race. As mentioned above, current U.S. Census reports classify Hispanics as being of any race, and established a reputable presumption that they are white. If this interpretation were let stand, America would soon become all Hispanic and we would be powerless to stop it. Hispanics

have Central and South America to return to, so unless they have the ap-
prearance of the average American (whose ancestral home is either the British
Isles or Northwestern Europe), they should not be citizens and allowed to
live in America.

### (ii) Repatriation

The last sentence in Section 2 of the draft twenty-seventh amendment which
reads, "only citizens shall have the right and privilege to reside permanently in the United States" will, in effect, provide for the relocation and repatriation of the non-citizens. This sentence mentions both the "right" and
"privilege" to reside permanently in the United States. If the sentence made
no mention of the word "privilege" and only provided that citizens have
the "right" to reside in the United States, the result might be a court ruling
that even though the non-citizens would not have the right under the Constitution to live in the United States, they would have the privilege to stay
by virtue of their presence here and the harshness of repatriation. Such a
ruling would defeat the purpose of much of the amendment and would result
in the continued growth of nonwhites who would not be citizens and would
brood ill-contentedly until their numbers made them powerful enough to
force change. The most sensible and prudent way to solve the problem of
race would be to institute a comprehensive and fair program of emigration,
so that all nonwhites can be repatriated in a manner that is economically
beneficial to them. Section 3 of the draft twenty-seventh amendment would
provide the foundation for this program.

Section 3 of this amendment reads: "The Congress and the several states,
except where expressly preempted by the Congress, shall have concurrent
power to enforce the provisions of this article by appropriate legislation in
coordination with the President as such legislation concerns the making of
treaties pursuant to Article 2, Section 2 of the Constitution."

This places the responsibility and authority to enforce the provisions of
the amendment with both the states and the legislative and executive bran-
chesof the federal government. This approach provides for the most flexibility and safeguards in enforcing the amendment. Concurrent power vested
in the states minimizes the possibility of undue intervention by an activist
judiciary on the one hand and systematic injustice by the central government on the other. Unjust action by the states could be checked by express
preemption by Congress. And all action for enforcement would be in coordination with the President.

An alternative approach would be to empower only Congress to enforce this article. To empower Congress only would be to ensure uniformity throughout the states but with the possibility of it being uniformly repressive. To empower the states as well will permit flexibility according to each state's circumstances. Moreover, since, as we will see below, the reponsibility for the proposal and ratification of this amendment will rest with the states, they will be more likely to act if they are given power to handle the problem directly and in a manner they deem appropriate. In any event, ultimate uniformity is ensured due to the guarantee of express preemption by Congress in this area. Further, since repatriation will involve dealing with foreign countries, states by themselves cannot negotiate directly with them. Accordingly, the states would defer to the policies and treaties established by the President in handling the aspects of the amendment which concern foreign states.

It should be understood that under proper procedure, repatriation can be effected in a fair and minimally painless manner. America possesses the capability to make every person's return easier and more rewarding than their original trip to these shores. The money that America now spends in social programs to solve the problems created by our new multiracial society can be spent to uproot a major source of these problems with as little pain as possible. Great sums of money can be used to provide repatriation allowances to the noncitizens returning to their homelands. Aid can be extended to their homelands to provide more efficient industries, broader job opportunities and more comfortable housing than our inner city ghettos now afford.

The entire process of repatriation could be done over a very long period of time if it should be determined that this would be the best approach and would provide for a smoother transition for all peoples concerned. The entire process could take thirty years if such time is necessary.

Once actual repatriation is accomplished other programs related thereto could be performed at leisure, such as guest worker permits for those who have been repatriated, continued repatriation compensation, and continued employment opportunities with the United States Government in this country and abroad, such as through military service. These programs could extend for many years into the future until all problems and hardships of repatriation are resolved.

Upon ratification of the amendment, the President and Congress could begin negotiations with the homelands to arrange for smooth repatriation. Each country could be dealt with separately and arrangements negotiated according to that country's particular needs, requirements, and obligations to the United States. At the same time negotiations are being conducted with the various homelands, the United States could begin requiring the repatriation of all those who can be readily repatriated, such as illegal aliens, persons of dual citizenship, permanent residents and citizens of U.S. trust territories. Non-immigrant residents with valid non-immigrant visas need not be affected because they will return home as their purpose for being in America is fulfilled.

Congress and the states could set a period of time by which all easily repatriatable nonwhites are to leave the country of their own volition. A one-year period of time could be sufficient. A determination could be made according to the facts as to which groups are easily repatriatable and, during this one-year period, the nonwhites so classified as easily repatriatable can, if they desire, liquidate their belongings, sell their homes, gather their possessions together and relocate. They need not sell their property if they do not desire to do so. They may retain title and rent or operate their businesses *in absentia*. They would have that choice and a period of time to make all necessary arrangements. Former citizens that voluntarily leave can be paid generous relocation allowances depending upon many factors such as need, length of time in America, economic level of the country they are returning to, etc., and they may be given priority to receive guest worker permits to return to the United States to work for a few years' duration at a time. During this one-year period, the government can assist in all ways possible, such as by the purchase of homes that are not easily marketable, providing subsidized transportation and financing the construction of additional housing in the homelands.

After the expiration of the one-year voluntary repatriation period, stricter yet fair measures could be taken to accomplish repatriation. If the Mexicans, for example, have not returned to their country, they could be rounded up and promptly returned across the border and their belongings could be confiscated as a penalty and to help defray the administrative costs. Forced repatriation could begin at this point. The ones who can most easily be repatriated will be, either swiftly and decisively or gradually and methodically, as the situation dictates. Those whose homelands are unwilling to take them may be allowed to stay on a temporary basis in temporary quarters until relocation can be accomplished. With certain adjustments, Hawaii could become a comfortable layover station for them. Below is a general discussion of how each group might be dealt with to effect the fairest and most efficient repatriation possible:

*Blacks.* Due to the large numbers and deep roots in the United States, it is toward this group that the United States should give the most consideration and allot the largest sums of money in order to ensure as pleasant a repatriation and new life as possible. Moreover, for these reasons, this group will be the most difficult to repatriate effectively and in good faith. The ideal situation would be for Southern African whites to accept U.S. citizenship in return for admitting U.S. blacks into their countries and allowing them to establish their own homelands. In this manner, the racial problems of several nations can be more easily resolved. Tribal problems within the homelands might still remain, and conflicts between blacks repatriated from the United States and local blacks might develop, but those problems can be dealt with in Africa just like national diverstity of whites has been dealt with in America. Moreover, an entirely new nation can be established in Africa where the blacks can build their own society. With the current educational level of U.S. blacks and their growing number of professionally trained men and women, this is indeed possible.

We must guarantee to the blacks a rich dowry to enable them to prosper in their homeland. Their U.S. education and culture combined with the economic support of America should make them valued citizens of their own or any number of African countries. African problems of illiteracy can be combatted by the U.S.-educated and repatriated blacks, and concepts of birth control and democracy will greatly be furthered in Africa through their influence.

In addition, blacks should be given first priority to guest worker permits to enable them to return to the U.S. for a few years at a time, or work for the U.S. Government abroad to earn more money to send back to their homeland and families. Even after repatriation, blacks could still continue to serve in our armed forces in the United States and throughout the world. They could serve in any number of positions in the United States. They could even serve as policemen stationed in U.S. cities for several years at a time. Once relocation is settled, the U.S. government should spare no expense in building fine accommodations for the returning blacks. Black labor can be employed to do this, with the end result being full employment for the blacks and housing that is superior to their current ghetto shelters. This difficult problem of repatriating blacks can most easily be solved now while Africa is still underpopulated in many regions. Negotiations with South Africa are possible at this point in time but may not be in the future. South Africa still maintains administrative control over such possible relocation areas as Nambia and Botswana. As time passes, the chances of dealing with the problem of repatriation of the blacks will become increasingly difficult and ultimately impossible.

*Hispanics.* Because of the large numbers of Hispanics in this country and the political instability in their mother countries, repatriation of this group could also be problematic. The vast majority of them can be dealt with simply by returning them to Mexico or elsewhere in Central America or the Carribean where they or their parents came from illegally. Generally they should not be greatly compensated for their repatriation unless they were legitimate citizens and then the compensation should be in proportion to their period of stay in the United States. Those who could, but would not, return home voluntarily within the initial one-year period would have their opportunity to take advantage of U.S. government largesse and programs curtailed. In any event, foreign aid to Mexico would be appropriate to help them relocate their citizens.

The Puerto Ricans should be returned to Puerto Rico. They should be able to return within the initial one-year period since it is a U.S. trust territory. Those who comply by returning to their homeland within the one-year period can be given opportunities to obtain guest worker permits. If they do not return to Puerto Rico within the one-year period, strict action could be taken. Puerto Rico may become crowded from repatriation. Accordingly, aid to alleviate the problems may be appropriate there. They should be schooled on the necessity of birth control prior to their return so that overcrowding of their country can be dealt with. Many other countries, such as China and South Korea, are at various stages of strict birth control campaigns which are proving most successful. Puerto Ricans, Mexicans and other Hispanics should learn from these experiences and adopt "one child" or other birth control campaigns of their own. Firmly encouraging responsible breeding habits could be the best thing for these countries and peoples.

Central Americans should be returned to Central America, Cubans to Cuba and the Carribean. However, if repatriation to Cuba is not immediately possible in light of current political conditions there, other Latin American countries should be encouraged to take them. If it appears that peoples' lives would be imminently imperiled by repatriation, then less expeditious action is advisable.

Hispanic whites who are basically indistinguishable from Americans whose ancestral home is the British Isles or Northwestern Europe, need not be repatriated. They should assimilate into the white society without turning our country into an extension of Latin America.

It should be noted that repatriation has become necessary primarily because of the abuses that the Hispanics have made of our system. They have come in illegally by the tens of millions and once they become citizens they use their influence and power to manipulate the system to protect their illegal alien countrymen. This nation is on the brink of becoming a Latin American nation. Strict action must be taken to avert this occurrence. Accordingly, stricter standards for citizenship are applied to them than to any other group. They must meet both the percentage tests and the appearance test for citizenship, otherwise they must be returned to Latin America.

*Orientals.* Orientals, as a whole, have not been in America very long or in large numbers. There are some who have been here several generations but, by and large, the bulk of the Oriental population in America has immigrated after the racial quotas were lifted in the 1960s. Accordingly, the first generation Orientals can be repatriated fairly easily along with their children for they might still claim citizenship in their mother country. They and their children will not have much culture shock or many adjustment problems. In addition, their English language skills will put them in valuable postitions in business when they return. It should be noted that Asia is the future center of world leadership and economic prosperity so repatriation for them should prove to be a blessing. Some Orientals will have a harder time returning than others. A breakdown is as follows:

*Chinese.* Many Chinese would not like to return to mainland China because of the communist regime there, even though it is rapidly liberalizing its policies and is developing into a strong, unified country with a considerable degree of freedom. Despite the fact that the numbers of U.S. Chinese are comparatively small, China may refuse to take them. On the other hand, China may be delighted to receive them and all the economic and educational wealth these repatriates could bring, together with their tangible wealth. China might very well treat them with great hospitality and give them special consideration. The attitude of China will remain an unknown factor until they express their own policy. In any event, with a little diplomatic pressure, homes could be found for them in Taiwan and Hong Kong or even in other countries with sizeable Chinese populations such as Malaysia, the Philippines, Vietnam or Cambodia.

*Japanese.* Generally, the U.S. Japanese have been longer residents of the United States than other Orientals except the Chinese. This length of time would make repatriation more difficult. Moreover, the United States has not been too successful recently in negotiation with the Japanese on even minor matters, much less major issues such as what repatriation would entail. If Japan says it does not want its countrymen back, then it will be difficult to force Japan to take them. The relatively new Japanese, the *issei* (first generation) or *nissei* would be more easily repatriated. Certainly the *issei* and the children of Japanese citizens who are still retained on the family registry in Japan could be repatriated without much difficulty because they would be Japanese citizens. Okinawa and the Ryukyu Islands might be a possible location for repatriation. Since that area of Japan was controlled by the United States until the 1960s, much English is spoken there, and American culture is prevalent. Ultimately, if negotiations did break down with Japan, we could negotiate with Russia to repatriate the Japanese to the USSR-controlled islands of Sakhalin which were Japanese possessions until World War II. Or we could negotiate with Brazil, which has a sizable Japanese settlement, and with various Asian countries.

*Filipinos.* The Filipinos are generally new arrivals, and many are still Philippine citizens. Accordingly, they can be repatriated without much difficulty. The Philippine government can be encouraged to assist.

*Koreans.* The Korean immigrants are also new and should be repatriated fairly easily. The South Korean government may not want to take them back since it might feel it cannot adequately employ them. Nevertheless, most Koreans in America were born in Korea and so can be repatriated there without confronting major obstacles. This is because they would still be listed in the family registry and can thereby more easily regain citizenship, if they ever lost it. If South Korea does not want the U.S. Koreans, North Korea might take them. The threat of sending the U.S.-resident Koreans to North Korea alone would be enough to encourage South Korea to be receptive. If the North Koreans do take them, it just may be good for the region. They may be able to teach Marshall Il-Sung Kim and his followers some principles of democracy and help to unite the two countries again.

*Indochinese.* Our country has just admitted a large number of Chinese from Vietnam, and many Vietnamese, Cambodians, Laotians, etc., who have fled their problematic countries and are complicating ours. Their repatriation may be difficult, not from adjusting to the culture of their homeland because they have not abandoned that culture, but because of political problems. Nevertheless, negotiations with the governments in the area should make repatriation possible.

*Native Americans.* American Indians, Aleuts, and Hawaiians should be allowed to remain in America and not face relocation. They would not be citizens of the United States and so would have to maintain their residence on their tribal reservations, but they would be permitted to remain within the nation's boundaries. This is how the Constitution contemplated the situation concerning them. Orientals and South Pacific Islanders who were born in Hawaii will not be considered Hawaiian just because they were born there.

*Peoples of Mixed Parentage.* According to the suggested amendment, persons of mixed parentage will not be citizens and will thereby be subject to repatriation to the country of their nonwhite parent. Where this is feasible, it should be done. Where it is not, certain alternative arrangments could be made.

Some flexibility may be necessary when working out the details of repatriation of those of mixed race and those nonwhites who are married to whites. For those of mixed race, it may at times be difficult to determine to which country they are to be repatriated. Factors to be considered are the desires of the individuals, the willingness of the homeland to accept them and the cultures with which they predominantly associate themselves. As for part-whites, it may not be practicable, at times, to return them to the country of their nonwhite origin. Action should be taken to effect repatriation where possible, particularly where the part-white is single. Individuals with a preponderance of white blood, but less than the statutory requirement for citizenship, and no Negro blood, who are nearly white in appearance might possibly be allowed to stay with their spouses in Hawaii, not as citizens, but under some legal fiction, such as granting them renewable guest worker permits, but requiring them to leave the United States every few years for brief durations to comply with the amendment's requirement that only citizens have the right to permanent residency.

For example, a Chinese whose mother is Chinese and father is white might be repatriated to China without many diplomatic or other problems. But a person who has three white grandparents and one Chinese grandparent may not. China might say the individual's Chinese blood is too diluted. Accordingly, Hawaii might become an acceptable residence for the individual.

In addition, since the repeal of the various state miscegenation statutes in the 1950s and 1960s and the breakdown of social taboos against interracial marriage, this nation has seen a rise in interracial couples. It should not be the policy of the nation to break up marriages, even interracial ones. Whites who are married to nonwhites should be encouraged to accompany their nonwhite spouse to his or her homeland. The fact that a nonwhite is married to a white should not, however, enable the nonwhite to remain in America. Such a ruling might cause a dramatic increase in interracial marriages as a means of nonwhites maintaining residence in the United States. Repatriation of nonwhites married to whites should, in the end, be effected.

The issue of interracial marriage would be indirectly dealt with by the suggested amendment. Since nonwhites would not be allowed to reside in the United States, interracial marriages would be impractical and may be proscribed by state law. The white spouse and the offspring of such a union would have to ultimately return to the homeland of the nonwhite spouse. If states allow interracial marriage at all, proof of this intention and the ability to effect that intention should be provided for such a union to occur. If certain accommodations are made for persons of mixed parentage to reside in Hawaii, miscegenation statutes can be drafted as necessity dictates.

*Miscellaneous Groups.* America has recently acquired a number of non-Mongoloid Asians, such as Iranians, Egyptians, Armenians, Turks, Arabs, Jews, Indians from India, Pakistanis, etc. It has also admitted Polynesians, such as Samoans and Tongans. In the last twenty years, America has become racially jumbled and unification will be tortuous. These peoples should be repatriated to their respective countries. America must stand firm for the first time in several generations.

In spite of the above recommendations for repatriation, America can be flexible in the implementation of its plan. Even so, as a whole we must remain resolute in our decisions. The following are some examples of some areas where flexibility might be available to the Congress or the states.

Questions arise as to what to do about those who cannot be easily repatriated at the initial stages. Such individuals could be granted provisional extensions to stay in America on a temporary basis until the situation changes and arrangements can be made for repatriation. Of course such an arrangement could be easily subject to abuses. Many individuals might try to use the excuse that their repatriation constitutes hardship in an attempt to remain in the United States. People may be inconvenienced in relocating, but that should not constitute grounds for granting a provisional extension to each of them. This arrangement should be reserved only for the extreme cases with possibly some sort of centralized waiting place like Hawaii where they can work and be productive but not make plans to stay permanently.

Another area of possible flexibility could be concerning nonwhite middle-aged and senior citizens. To repatriate them could be more than a mere inconvenience—it could be extremely burdensome on them in their old age. To require them to start life anew at age 50, 60, or 70 is not a necessary step in the overall scheme of retaining America for the Americans. They are past the age where they will bear children and so would not leave a lasting effect on the racial makeup of the nation. These individuals whose children are grown and who wish to stay in America could be allowed to do so under some special arrangement worked out by the states or by Congress.

Nothing to this effect should be written into the constitutional amendment because of the danger of the judicial branch abusing and defeating the purpose of the amendment through misinterpretation of any written exceptions. Instead, states or Congress could devise some sort of legal fiction to allow the non-citizen elderly to stay in America. For example, the government might issue renewable ten-year residence permits to those individuals over age 60 who would be adversely affected by the draft twenty-seventh amendment.

When contemplating the actual repatriation, an obvious concern comes to mind as to whether such can be carried out without causing bloodshed and civil war. It would be tragic if lives were lost due to disobedience. Such occurrences must be avoided at all reasonable costs. The surest way to avoid such violence is to be very strict in the enforcement of the process and allow no deviation from the guidelines established by the appropriate governments.

The group most prone to violent disobedience could be the blacks. This necessitates specific consideration to ensure compliance. One way to do this would be to designate and hire them to be the policing force for the amendment. Because of their physical abilities, the blacks would be the ideal enforcers as against other blacks as well as the rest of the nation. If they play a major role in the enforcement of the amendment, opposition and violent reaction would be greatly reduced.

The average black could be enticed to the job of enforcing the amendment once he becomes convinced that it is inevitable and not terribly disadvantageous to him. Generous monetary rewards could be an alluring factor to his enlistment. In addition to the money, were he promised guest worker permits in the United States, after repatriation is complete, and a good job, plus security in his new country, he could probably improve his station in life through the amendment. When the prospect of the black man sinking lower on the economic charts due to the influx of more successful nonwhite immigrants is combined with the fact that these immigrants are often more discriminatory toward the blacks than the whites ever were, the young black man may be eager to assist in the enforcement of the amendment.

The blacks would render one final service to America which would indeed be the service that saved it from ruin. Accordingly, America should be profoundly grateful and make compensation. Repatriation could thereby be carried out in an orderly fashion. Care must be taken, however, to ensure that the enforcers do not become overzealous in their duties.

In sum, repatriation is a viable option, one that can be carried out systematically, intelligently, and with little more than inconvenience to a few groups in our society. The end result will be a more harmonious environment for all. Both blacks and whites will be better-off. The Orientals will return to countries that are the new world leaders and have the brightest futures and the illegal aliens will finally end up in their own countries.

We must realize that peoples often migrate and change countries, cultures and residences. Nonwhite Americans will not be that impositioned by repatriation. For many, there will be less than a six-month adjustment. The illegal aliens and first-generation immigrants might not even be inconvenienced for that long. For others, the process may take as long as five years until they fully adjust. In any case, if America is determined to make repatriation as pleasant and positive an experience as possible, many could be much better-off even at the outset and all will be better-off in the long run.

Each of us probably has several friends and acquaintances who will be seemingly adversely affected by this amendment. Therefore it will be easy for us to become caught up in our concern for our friends to such an extent that we forget about the overall effect massive nonwhite immigration is having on our country. Our love and concern for our friends must not prevent us from doing what is right and best for our country. We must realize that they will get along fine under the new adjustments and be able to succeed in their new situation. Our love and concern for our nonwhite friends and acquaintances should encourage us to act for the ratification of the amendment and for the institution of fair procedures to protect all our interests.

Due to our current cultural conditioning, the entire concept of repatriation may seem harsh and wrong to a great many people. These people may earnestly hope for what is best for America, but feel that the hardships of repatriation are not worth the benefits that would accrue to America therefrom. It must be realized that if we take measures now and institute a fair and administratively sound program for repatriation, countless hardship and pain in the future can be avoided. If we take action now, we will inconvenience a few people, but if we do not take action, we will allow a crisis to develop within our boundaries. Once the nonwhites become the majority, or even before that when they become a very large minority, they will naturally take away more of the rights of the Americans. Racial conflict will escalate and an oppressive and destructive race war will threaten as a distinct possibility. The racial imbalance of our nation will not only result in our being displaced by nonwhites due to their numbers and voting strength, but will very likely result in the violent deaths of many Americans from armed clashes. Violent race war need not break out. Whites could, as an alternative, give the mantle of authority over to the nonwhites without a challenge. We can continue to cede them political, economic, educational and social power little by little as we are doing now until they at last have the entire share of America's wealth. This could result in few and only scattered violent conflicts as have been happening in recent years. To many, this possibility may be a brighter outlook than the possibility of race war. However, most peoples do not want to give away their country nor effect harsh measures so they deceive themselves into thinking the freedom of the whites will be protected even when they are a minority in the United States—a misconception that will prove fatal.

In the long run, the inevitable inconvenience and hardships the amendment will impose on portions of the nonwhite population is the better alternative. A little inconvenience now to a few people is better than the breakdown and collapse of our system and nation resulting in many deaths and much hardship which will surely result if no action is taken. We can ensure that justice is served if we control repatriation and our country. We can ensure nothing if we relinquish that control. We will not even be able to secure a place in which our children can raise their families.

### (c) Ratification

Section 4 of the draft twenty-seventh amendment provides for its own ratification as follows: "This article shall be inoperative unless it shall have been ratified as an amendment to the Constitution by the Legislatures of three-fourths of the several states within seven years of its submission."

Beginning with the eighteenth amendment, Congress has customarily included a provision requiring ratification within seven years from the time of the submission to the States. The U.S. Supreme Court in *Coleman v. Miller*,[456] declared that the question of the reasonableness of the time within which a sufficient number of States must act is a political question to be determined by Congress. Accordingly, establishing a seven-year limitation for ratification will insure that the period of time for ratification is not an issue. It should be remembered, however, that pursuant to Article V of the Constitution the method of ratification, whether by the state legislatures or by state convention, is left to the discretion of the Congress. Accordingly, a constitutional convention which proposes the twenty-seventh amendment may not propose Section 4; only Congress may pass on this method of ratification.

# VII. THE CONVENTION METHOD OF AMENDING THE U.S. CONSTITUTION

## 1. Overview

Article V of the U.S. Constitution provides that:

> The Congress, whenever two thirds of both Houses shall deem it necessary, shall propose Amendments to this Constitution, or on the Application of the Legislatures of two thirds of the several States, shall call a Convention for proposing Amendments, which, in either Case, shall be valid to all Intents and Purposes, as Part of this Constitution, when ratified by the Legislatures of three fourths of the several States, or by Conventions in three fourths thereof, as the one or the other Mode of Ratification may be proposed by the Congress; Provided that . . . no State, without its Consent, shall be deprived of its equal Suffrage in the Senate.

The above-quoted Article V provides that amendments to the Constitution may be proposed either by Congress or by a convention called for that same purpose. In addition, it provides that Congress shall determine whether ratification is to be accomplished by the state legislatures or by state conventions. When ratified by three-fourths of the state legislatures or state conventions, an amendment becomes part of the Constitution. In all cases, amendments have been proposed by Congress, that is to say, no convention has ever been held to propose amendments, and in all but one case (the twenty-first amendment enacted to repeal prohibition), the amendments have been ratified by state legislatures rather than by state conventions. The convention method of proposing amendments has never been employed because two-thirds of the states have never applied for a convention to propose amendments dealing with the same general subject matter.[457] However, in March 1967, Congress had received applications from thirty-two states (two applications shy of the requisite thirty-four states) requesting a convention to propose an amendment which would overrule the U.S. Supreme Court's reapportionment decisions.[458]

State legislatures have often mounted convention campaigns when they have been dissatisfied with the action of the various branches of the federal government.[459] The purpose of the convention method of proposing amendments is to provide an alternative to the proposal of amendments by Congress in order to ensure that the states could correct congressional abuses of power or propose amendments which Congress refused to propose.[460]

In light of the attitude of the present Congress and because of the sensitive nature of this potentially explosive proposal, it is unlikely that the Congress would propose on its own an amendment such as the one suggested. Accordingly, the procedure for the ratification of this amendment will develop by the alternative amendment process. In other words, proposal of the amendment by Congress will be forgone in favor of proposal by constitutional convention.

There are advantages to proposing the amendment through constitutional convention. The most important one is that it can be achieved without Congress' consent or support. By the convention process, the state legislatures can force Congress to submit the suggested amendment to the states. Even though the convention method is likely to take a long time, it can be accomplished in a speedier and simpler manner than much of Congress' action which can take years before becoming law. A delegation to the convention, actually appointed by the states to further the purposes of the suggested amendment can work in unison, whereas Congress may be factionalized. Moreover, by the time the convention proposes the amendment, the battle for ratification will almost be won because the states will have already acted in unison, which is the most important step in the ratification process. A disadvantage of the constitutional convention approach is that in practice it has never been done, so binding guidelines are almost nonexistent. Rules governing procedure will have to be established once the requisite number of petitions have been filed with Congress. This chapter takes into consideration the problem of the lack of rules and procedures. Measures will hereinafter be suggested to help clarify and simplify the constitutional convention approach to amending the Constitution.

Even if Congress would consider proposing an amendment such as the one suggested herein, it is certain to be bogged down by opposition at every step because of its volatile and polemic nature. At the local government level, however, as opposed to the congressional level, swift action might be possible. Because of the relative unity of the people there, proposals can be made and adopted with a minimal amount of friction and frustration by special interest groups. When most everyone in a town thinks alike, politics work the smoothest and the best. The alternative amendment process is based on this theory. Support at the local levels for this proposal, directed towards local legislatures, can result in quick action and the chance to reestablish our standards of conduct and preserve our racial identity. Theoretically, the states acting together may, in effect, create, propose, and ratify an amendment to the Constitution without any more than the nominal participation of Congress. States themselves can deliberate and decide what is best for themselves and the nation without having to work through a short-sighted Congress.

State legislatures, often comprised of part-time legislators who serve their country in their spare time for the purpose of furthering democracy rather than full-time politicians who, at times, tend to be more concerned about the future of their careers than the future of the nation, would be able to swiftly move to make this amendment the law of the land. Large states like California and New York which are already so factionalized that positive action would be difficult to achieve could remain in their disorganized condition and not hamper or even affect the political process in Wyoming or Arkansas. Moreover, as will be discussed below, each state, regardless of its size, might have equal say in the process of proposing the amendent and have equal say in its ratification.

Applications of two-thirds (or thirty-four) of the states are required to successfully petition Congress for a constitutional convention under Article V to propose the amendment. Once that number is reached, only four more states would need to join to ratify the amendment proposed by the thirty-four and thereby make it operative. By action of only thirty-eight states, the precipitous decline of our standards of conduct and slide toward a nonwhite majority can be averted. America has a cushion of twelve states who need not act. These twelve states may very well be the largest and the most racially and morally diverse and who fail to act because of pressure from various interest groups; or they may be small, homogenous states who cannot see the threat. Twelve states is a sufficiently large margin to work with and makes ratification a possibility through unified effort of the thirty-eight. The alternate amendment process may well prove difficult and lengthy especially considering the fact that some state legislatures meet only once every two years[461] making immediate action by those state legislatures nearly impossible.

In addition, the convention itself could last for well over a year, although, a shorter period of time is possible. In the last two decades there have been proposed in Congress bills entitled "Constitutional Convention Procedures

Act," commonly known as the Ervin Bill and the Helms Bill[462] that have, at times, received Senate approval but have not been acted upon by the House. The Helms Bill, for example, imposes a time limit on the deliberations of the convention: ordinarily the convention shall "terminate" one year after the date of the first meeting.[463] Constitutional conventions convened by the states of Alaska (1956) and New Jersey (1966) have lasted only two months or so.[464] Connecticut's convention of 1965 lasted four months.[465] However, the length of Rhode Island's convention was two years, meeting once a week.[466]

Moreover, the alternate amendment process will not even begin to have operation until the requisite thirty-four states have submitted petitions. Once the requisite number of petitions have been filed, then there commence the difficulties of initiating a process that has never been tried, has no guidelines, and that numerous legal commentators, scholars and congressmen have tried to thwart through a variety of legal theories detailed below. Once a convention is called and the suggested amendment is proposed, then those thirty-four states, plus an additional four must ratify the proposed amendment. At that point the amendment will become law, but still will not be beyond attack. Once the amendment becomes law, the courts might review the process and strike it down or give it no effect if the court deems that the process does not satisfy the requirements of Article V of the Constitution.[467]

In spite of these obstacles, the alternative amendment process can work and can be the means to effect the necessary changes in our society. Indeed, the alternative amendment process might be the only means possible to achieve these ends, since Congress probably could not be persuaded to propose an amendment such as this. Accordingly, only through a convention could this amendment be proposed to the states. If Congress does propose the suggested amendment, then there would be no need to call a convention to propose amendments, and the process will be simplified, but the assumption of this text is that Congress will not propose the suggested amendment and that the alternative amendment process is the only avenue available to effect change. Accordingly, this alternative amendment process to alter the Constitution by convention is detailed below. The problems, barriers, and the way to overcome them will also be discussed hereinafter.

The Founding Fathers agreed that the admittedly imperfect Constitution could preserve the young nation only if a means existed by which it could be supplemented or corrected.[468] James Madison, who attended the Philadelphia Convention as a delegate from Virginia wrote in *The Federalist*: "That useful alterations will be suggested by experience, could not but be foreseen. It was requisite, therefore, that a mode for introducing them be provided."[469] Professor John William Burgess, professor of history, political science and international law at Columbia University, concluded that the amendment clause forms "the most important part of a Constitution. Upon its existence and truthfulness, i.e., its correspondence with real and natural conditions, depends the question as to whether the state shall develop with peaceable continuity, or shall suffer alternations of stagnation, retrogression and revolution."[470]

"The convention alternative appears at first glance to be straightforward: upon application of the legislatures of two-thirds of the states, Congress shall call a convention for proposing amendments. If one is proposed, it must be made effective in the same way as a congressionally proposed amendment—by approval of conventions in three-fourths of the states or ratification by three-fourths of the state legislatures. Congress selects the required method of approval.

Further consideration reveals, however, that this restatement tells us virtually nothing about how the process actually would operate."[471]

The various steps to the convention alternative must be inferred from the procedure broadly delineated in Article V of the Constitution. These steps are as follows:

> The first step is "the Application of the Legislatures of two thirds of the several States" for a convention. After proper "Applications" are received, Congress, as the second step, "shall call a Convention for proposing Amendments." Incident to that "call," Congress will have to provide for the selection of delegates; choosing those delegates is the third step in the process. Then, as the fourth step, the convention meets. After the convention reports its proposals, Congress is called upon to take the fifth step: to select the "mode of Ratification" of the proposed amendments—ratification either by the "Legislatures of three-fourths of the several States" or by ratifying conventions in three-fourths of the states. The sixth and final step is the actual consideration of ratification in the states.[472]

Debate about an Article V convention exists at almost every step of the process. Legal scholars and legislatures are split in opinion over this area that has little law or precedent governing it. Opinions of the commentators on these issues are often influenced more by their political sentiments than by what the weight of authority or reason should be, with conservatives advocating positions which simplify the convention and liberals advocating positions which impede it. On the face, this constitutes an apparent paradox.

One would not think that the conservatives would advocate a process which would change the Constitution and the liberals oppose such change. It must be remembered, however, that the liberals have been quite successful in promoting their philosophies through activist interpretation of the Constitution. Liberal-leaning justices have effectively implemented their liberal programs by bending the Constitution to fit their ends. Conservatives, by and large, want to amend the Constitution to neutralize the actions of the liberals.

The importance of the debate over the convention process is made manifest when it is understood that high-powered opponents to the suggested amendment, such as judges and congressmen, might be able to thwart a constitutional convention, even if the requisite number of states call for one, by taking action that is excused through theories concocted more for the result they advocate than the reason they possess. The importance of the debate over the convention process is magnified when one realizes that even if all the barriers in the path of a convention are overcome, a convention is held, an amendment proposed and ratified by the states, today's U.S. Supreme Court, with its *de facto* legislative powers might find the amendment unconstitutional if it deemed that the convention process was not conducted in accordance with the steps inferred from Article V. As we shall see hereinafter, for each step in the process there are opposing opinions as to which is proper and constitutional. The convention can be held only by choosing one method or the other at each step. This means that at each step, the rejected method may be used by opponents of the amendment to attack the process on constitutional grounds, thereby affording the U.S. Supreme Court with theories to find that the process was conducted in an unconstitutional manner, if such be the end desire of the Court, regardless of the methods employed and regardless of whether or not the states desired the amendment, proposed it and ratified it.

In spite of these obstacles, the convention process is, by default, the desired course of action since it is unlikely that Congress would propose the suggested amendment on its own.

In order to fashion the convention process in a manner that is conducive to success in implementation while at the same time attempt to avoid judicial scrutiny and a finding of unconstitutionality, the issues of the debate over the convention process are set forth below as is a suggested course of action by the state legislatures that is based upon those issues.

## 2. Major Points of Debate Regarding the Six Steps to a Convention

A discussion of the major points of debate that concern the above-listed six steps of an Article V convention is as follows:

### (a) The Application of the Legislatures of Two-Thirds of the Several States

A resolution by a state legislature calling for a constitutional convention has been held to constitute a sufficient "application" to Congress within the requirements of Article V.[473] Accordingly, state legislatures should submit an application in this form. The issues concerning the application are set forth below:

### (i) Applications for Limited vs. Unlimited Conventions

"The most hotly debated question about the convention method has been whether the scope of a convention, or the state application for it, can be limited to a particular subject or must be general and undefined."[474] The premise of those who oppose the calling of a limited convention, such as Professor Charles Black of Yale Law School, is this: "Unless Congress concludes that thirty-four states have submitted resolutions contemplating an unrestricted convention for proposing amendments, Congress should decline to 'call a convention.' A qualified or limited or restricted state legislative resolution, one which would display an unwillingness to have the convention free to consider and to propose whatever amendments it deems appropriate to be submitted for possible ratification, should be regarded by Congress as falling short of the requisite commitment by that state. A 'qualified' application by a state legislature is, in contemplation of Article V, no sufficient application at all."[475]

According to Professor Black, the consequence of state petitions for a limited convention is: "Congress cannot be obligated, no matter how many states ask for it, to summon a convention for a limited purpose...alone, and that such a convention would have no constitutional standing at all."[476]

Regardless of Professor Black's position on the matter, the "states have assumed from the outset that limited applications are valid. They seem also to have assumed that the requisite number (two-thirds of the states) of limited applications will require that a resulting convention be similarly limited in scope. A 1974 tabulation of all state applications since 1789 indicated that only 18 of the 356 applications made in that 185-year period sought a general convention."[477]

Further, the Helms and Ervin Bills would provide that a convention may be limited to its subject matter and even require states to specify the subject matter of amendments to be proposed.[478] They may, however, call for an open convention but the Helms and Ervin Bills, as they were drafted, would not have governed in such instances had they become law.[479]

Under the Helms and Ervin Bills, the only applications that can be aggregated toward the two-thirds requirement are the ones that deal with the same subject matter.[480] The Senate Report from the Ervin Bill provided: "Whether applications seeking a convention for different reasons should be counted together toward the requisite two-thirds of the states is not at issue in this discussion, since it is undisputed that they should not be. The Senate Judiciary Committee noted that 'two centuries of practice' support the conclusion that a convention should not be called unless the application of two-thirds of the state legislatures deal with the same subject matter."[481]

This issue raises a related question: "Does Congress have any discretion under article V whether to call a convention? The language is mandatory, stating that when the applications are received Congress 'shall' call a convention. The question interposed by those arguing against the validity of limited applications is whether Congress has received valid applications, requiring a convention call, if the thirty-four applications contain limitations. If not, they argue, the mandatory language of article V is not triggered by limited applications, and Congress need not—in fact may not—call a convention. As Professor Black has summarized it, 'Thirty-four times zero is zero.' "[482]

In sum, in order to give Congress no discretion in calling a convention, the petitions by the state legislatures should not attempt to limit the subject matter of the convention but should specify the subject matter it wants the convention to propose.

### (ii) Governor's Veto Power Over the Applications by State Legislators

An additional question concerning the first step in the convention process, the application step, is whether a state governor has veto power over the legislature's application for an Article V Convention. Article V speaks of application by the "legislatures of the several States" and makes no mention of governors.[483] The U.S. Supreme Court in *Hawke v. Smith*[484] which stated as settled that "the submission of a constitutional amendment [does] not require the action of the President,"[485] held that the term "Legislature" in the context of legislative ratification of a federal constitutional amendment, means only that specific body itself, and not the states' lawmaking apparatus in general.[486]

Further, the Helms and Ervin Bills provides that in adopting a resolution to submit an application to Congress, a state legislature is to follow its normal procedures for passing a statute, except that the governor's approval is not required.[487] The Senate Report cites *Hawke v. Smith* as precedent to support the exclusion of governors from the application process[488] and as a policy reason states that a gubernatorial veto is just too high a hurdle for state legislatures to overcome.[489]

Professor Black, on the other hand, asserts that "the amendment process should not be made easy, and the inclusion in it of the governors of the states, popularly elected statewide, would be a desirable further check."[490]

Regardless of Professor Black's opinion, it does not appear that a resolution requires the signature of the governor of the state.[491] Because of the difficulty in overriding a gubernatorial veto, and since gubernatorial consent appears not to be required, the resolution to submit an application to call a convention to Congress should be in whatever technical form the state employs for a single resolution of both houses of the legislature which does not require the governor to approve or veto. If, however, the governor will approve the resolution, such an act might give more weight and support to the petition.

### (iii) Contemporaneity of Application

"Article V does not specify the time span within which applications must occur to spark a convention . . . . The text of Article V does not refer to a requirement of contemporaneity. I think it can fairly be inferred, however, that some general contemporaneity is necessary. The justaposition within article V of the convention method and the mechanism of congressional proposal provides textual support for the proposition that the two alternatives are somewhat parallel. Congressional proposal is, by definition, contemporaneous: all members vote at the same time. The state applications for a convention should evidence similarly widespread support and should be required to fall within some limited time span.    The Supreme Court's decision in *Dillon v. Gloss* supports the argument that a textually demonstrable requirement of contemporaneity pervades article V. In *Dillon* the Court upheld congressional power to set a time limit for ratification of congressionally proposed amendments. The Court reasoned that because article V treats proposal and ratification as 'succeeding steps in a single endeavor', the text implies that they may not be separated by any great length of time;

they must instead 'reflect the will of the people in all sections at relatively the same period.' If the text implies a requirement of contemporaneity between proposal and ratification, it must also imply contemporaneity for the various components—the state applications—of the alternative process by which a proposal may be initiated."[492]

Further, section 5 (a) of the Ervin and Helms Bills as they passed in the Senate provided that "an application...shall remain effective for seven calendar years after the date it is received by the Congress."[493] If the requisite number of states submit contemporaneous applications, and are not deemed to be defective for any other reason, then Congress is compelled by Article V to call a convention. The nearer the applications are to each other in time, the easier the issue of contemporaneity is resolved. Based upon precedent, seven years appears to be a reasonable length of time in which two-thirds of the states must submit applications. Certainly, any longer period of time will give Congress room to employ discretion whether or not to call a convention. A problem that might arise is if the accumulation of the requisite number of applications requires, say, five years. Some congressmen who do not approve of the amendment may aver, in spite of the above, that such a period is too long to satisfy the contemporaneity requirement. If a congressman does not want to call a convention, he will employ every means available to avoid being obligated under the Constitution to call a convention. Further, there exists a question, which will be discussed later, as to whether or not Congress can even be compelled to call a convention. Thus, it is very important for the state legislatures to act promptly and submit applications to Congress in as close a proximity of time to each other as possible.

### (iv) Withdrawal of an Application

The Helms and Ervin Bills provide that state legislatures are able to withdraw their applications.[494] Whether or not this would actually be possible is yet unclear. In the reapportionment drive in the 1960s, one state legislature made a purported withdrawal of its prior application after Congress had received thirty-two applications.[495] Had two more states submitted applications, Congress would have had to address the effect of the attempted withdrawal. Concerning the suggested amendment, if states withdraw their applications, Congress could most likely use it as a reason to not call the convention if it disagrees with the amendment's contents. Since Congress has a great deal of discretionary power in determining whether it is bound by Article V to call a convention, any legitimate grounds that will excuse Congress from calling a convention could be fatal to the calling of a convention.

## (b) After Proper Applications Are Received, Congress Shall Call a Convention

Two fundamental questions arise concerning the calling of a convention by Congress: (i) If Congress refuses to call a convention, can it be forced to do so; and (ii) does the President have a power of veto over the calling of a convention?

### (i) What if Congress Refuses to Call a Convention?

*American Jurisprudence*, the leading encyclopedia of U.S. law recites that opinion if Congress refuses to call a convention a federal court should compel Congress to do so. It states:[496]

> Article V provides that Congress, on the application of the legislatures of two-thirds of the several states, shall call a convention for proposing amendments. The Supreme Court has interpreted "shall" to mean "must," so that the duty of Congress to call a convention upon demand can properly be characterized as "ministerial." In such a case a federal court should give mandamus to one of the petitioning states to compel Congress to call the convention, although some writers have had doubts the judiciary would act. Such judicial assistance to a proper party plaintiff in no way violates the doctrine of separation of powers as properly understood. But Congress must of necessity decide whether the conditions exist which give rise to this duty, and it must decide whether applications for a convention are valid and when a sufficient number of states have petitioned for a convention.

The above quotation mentions that some writers feel that the judiciary would not act to compel Congress to call a convention. A summary of this rationale is as follows:[497]

> The Supreme Court has applied the "political question" doctrine to a broad range of cases in holding actions of the legislative or executive branch of government conclusive on the courts. When the Court deems a political question to be involved in a case, it does not merely give the political branches broad discre-

tion; it rules the issue entirely nonjusticiable.

It has been argued that any determination of Congress related to the amending process constitutes such a political question.

The Ervin and Helms Bills provide that determinations made by Congress regarding the procedural sufficiency of state applications, rescissions, and ratifications shall be "binding on all others, including State and Federal Courts."[498] Even if this Bill had become law, it is possible that the courts would ignore it. As Professor Black stated: "It seems to me clear beyond doubt, on the most fundamental principles of *Marbury v. Madison*, that no court, state, or federal can be coerced by Congress into acting on the basis of an amendment which that court believes has not the force of law, where that court conscientiously concluded, as a matter of law, that the tendered issue is justiciable."[499]

If Congress refuses to call a convention even though the requisite number of states have submitted proper applications, it is unclear whether the judiciary will order Congress to do so. Since officials in all branches of government are bound by oath to uphold the Constitution, the Executive Branch might be justified in taking some sort of action to force Congress to call a convention. However, there is no precedent for the President to take such action. Further, it is conceivable that the court could give mandamus to a petitioning state, rule that the applications are proper and order Congress to call a convention. Whereupon, Congress could claim that only it, and not the courts, possesses the right to determine the properness of the application and ignore the court ruling. What would happen in the event of such a stalemate between the courts and Congress is unclear and is without precedent.

In sum, it should be noted that, regardless of the wording of Article V, Congress possesses a great deal of discretionary power. Therefore, unless the applications are proper in every respect and above challenge as far as possible, Congress might not feel obligated to call a convention, and the states might have no recourse.

### (ii) Does the President Have a Power of Veto Over the Calling of a Convention?

Article V makes no mention whether or not the President can veto a congressional call for a convention.[500] Article I, Section 7, of the Constitution provides that "Every Order, Resolution, or Vote to which the Concurrence of the Senate and House of Representatives may be necessary (except on a question of Adjournment) shall be presented to the President" for his approval or veto.[501]

However, the Senate Report of the Ervin Bill "concluded that Presidential participation in the operation of Article V is not required by the Constitution. Indeed, a strong case is made out that the Constitution, as construed throughout our history, precludes such participation by the Executive in the amendment process."[502] It stated that Article I, Section 7 did not apply to Congressional actions in the amendment process because the function performed by Congress in this process does not require making legislative judgments but rather merely providing the machinery by which the desires of the state can be effectuated.[503]

The U.S. Supreme Court had considered the analogous question whether congressionally proposed amendments are subject to Presidential veto. In *Hollingsworth v. Virginia*,[504] the Court rejected a challenge of the constitutionality of the eleventh amendment, which had not been submitted to the President. The Court stated: "The negative of the president applies only to the ordinary cases of legislation; he has nothing to do with the proposition or adoption of amendments to the constitution."[505] As stated above, in 1920, the Court in *Hawke v. Smith* stated as settled that "the submission of a constitutional amendment [does] not require the action of the President."[506]

In spite of this weight of authority, scholars have criticized the exclusion of the President in the amendment process as being contrary to a literal reading of Article I, Section 7 which requires presidential approval of any congressional action having the force of law. In response to the Ervin Bill, Professor Black stated: "The exclusion of the President from the process of calling a convention is flatly and obviously unconstitutional under Article I, Section 7, and the only question about this is how 'strict constructionists' could espouse such a position."[507] He asserts that the calling of a convention would have the force of law much as legislation and is properly subject to the presidential veto.[508]

It is important to note that in the context of a calling of a convention, "the President has no meaningful role to perform. The President, like Congress, would not be free to interfere with the amendment process if constitutional requirements had been met, regardless of his views on the constitutional changes sought by the states. The only important contribution to the process which the President might provide would be to ensure that Congress had acted consistently with article V. But the need for review of these constitutional questions by another political branch is doubtful, since the courts, the government branch primarily responsible for constitutional interpretation and protection will not give effect to amendments which have not satisfied the requirements of article V."[509]

A major drawback in affording the President veto power over the calling of a convention is that he "could probably find some constitutional pretext for blocking any amendment with whose substance he disagreed, and Congress might not be able to muster the two-thirds vote necessary to override his veto.[510]

The issue of whether or not the President has a veto power over the calling of a convention is not one to be decided by the state legislatures in their petitions. The most that they can do is submit a memorial to Congress and the President along with their petition requesting that the President not attempt, or be allowed to attempt, to veto the convention.

### (c) Choosing Convention Delegates

### (i) State Choice vs. Congress Direction

The Constitutional Convention Implementation Act of 1979, a version of the Helms and Ervin Bills, proposed by Senator Oren Hatch provides: "Each state shall appoint [delegates], in such manner as the legislature thereof may direct."[511] Even though this bill is not law, it demonstrates that Congress feels it has the constitutional power to prescribe the procedure for the selection of delegates.

To me it is unclear that Congress does have that power. The language of Article V does not assign this responsibility to Congress. Further, the method of selecting the delegates to the original Constitutional Convention, which drafted Article V, was not prescribed by the Continental Congress. A logical reading of the tenth amendment should act to reserve such procedures to the states. State legislatures would submit applications for a convention only if Congress is unresponsive to their desires. Accordingly, neither they nor the Founding Fathers would want an unresponsive Congress to prescribe the method of selecting delegates. It would defeat the purpose if, under the rubric "procedure," Congress could cause the states to stack their delegations with individuals who would obstruct amendments when Congress disagreed with their substance.

The Ervin Bill and the Helms Bill provide for the number of delegates to be equal to the whole number of Senators and Representatives to which the state may be entitled in Congress.[512] This method would make the convention very large in number and unwieldly in action. In order to help ensure that state legislatures are able to determine their own method of selecting delegates, state legislatures should include in their memorial to Congress to accompany their application, the request that Congress shall instruct the states to appoint delegates in a manner the state legislatures shall direct.

It is easier to conclude that, arising from its duty to call a convention, Congress has more of a right to designate the number of delegates and their apportionment among the states than to direct how the states are to appoint their delegates. Where the method of appointing delegates is strictly an internal matter for the states, the number that they send to the convention concerns every other state.

The original Ervin Bill allowed each state only as many delegates as the state had Representatives in Congress (excluding Senators)[513] thus calling for one hundred less delegates than its successor bills. If convention voting is done by state bloc, the fewer the delegates the better. Not only will fewer delegates be able to reach agreement more easily, but they will also be less likely to propose amendments which do not deal with the subject matter for which the convention was called. In any event, since each state would have a single vote, the more populous states would not have a larger voice even if they sent more delegates. (It is assumed that the more populous states would be less likely to support the suggested amendment because of their current racial composition.)

If convention voting is by individual delegate, delegate apportionment should, at the very least, be based on the states' representation in both the Senate and the House, thereby giving the less populous states more of a voice in the convention than if apportionment were based on Representatives in Congress only.

A problem faced by states which are in favor of the suggested amendment when they petition Congress is whether to request Congress to apportion the delegates according to Representatives in Congress or according to Representatives and Senators in Congress, since, at the time of petition, they cannot be sure whether the convention voting will be based upon state bloc or individual delegate. Therefore, they cannot be sure which method will be the most conducive to proposing the amendment. Accordingly, in their memorial to Congress to accompany their application, the states should recommend to Congress that each state send a certain number of delegates, regardless of population or representation in Congress.

At the original Constitutional Convention, Virginia sent only these delegates: George Washington, James Madison, and Edmund Randolph.[514] With men of that stature, why send more? If each state sent three delegates, that would be 150 delegates, a large enough body for any convention, but small enough for efficiency. Each state in its memorial should suggest that each state choose three delegates to the Constitution.

### (d) Convention Procedure

### (i) Congressional Claim to Substantive Role in Setting Convention Procedure

As the fourth step in the alternate amendment process, the convention meets. Article V gives no indication of how a convention would be run, nor does it assign responsibility for this determination. Certain writers assert that Congress is empowered to prescribe those "housekeeping matters" which are necessary aspects of the implementation of Congress' duty to call a convention.[515]

In the Ervin and Helms Bills, Congress inferred it must regulate the convention procedure based upon the "necessary and proper" clause of the Constitution[516] which allows Congress to select the means necessary to perform its duties,[517] and "because states which appl[y] for a convention [can] not be expected to formulate procedures for it . . . . "[518] Certain legal scholars, however, believe that Congress does not have the right to regulate convention procedure. Professor Gunther of Stanford Law School states:[519]

> In my view, the text, history and structure of Article V make a congressional claim to play a substantial role in setting the agenda of the convention highly questionable. If the state-initiated method for amending the Constitution was designed for anything, it was designed to minimize the role of Congress. Congress was given only two responsibilities under that portion of Article V, and I believe that, properly construed, these are extremely narrow responsibilities. First, Congress must call the convention when thirty-four valid applications are at hand (and it is of course a necessary part of that task to consider the validity of the applications and to set up the machinery for convening the convention). Second, Congress has the responsibility for choosing a method of ratification once the convention submits its proposals. I am convinced that is all that Congress can properly do.
>
> I suspect that the Ervin-Helms effort at congressional guardianship over the scope of the convention's deliberations rests on the mistaken assumption that the approach of *McCulloch v. Maryland*—the view of broad discretionary powers of Congress so familiar in other circumstances—is appropriate to congressional action under Article V. True, the Necessary and Proper Clause applies to all powers of Congress; but the scope of the implementing powers surely turns on the nature of the underly-

ing authority and its context in the Constitution. The delineation of congressional authority regarding the convention route must heed the fact that it is a route largely intended to bypass Congress, to place the initiative for beginning the process in the states, and to give the central role in the proposing of amendments to the constitutional convention itself.

Accordingly, if the requisite states submit a memorial to Congress to accompany their application, stating a uniform request concerning the method of voting and the percentage required to propose an amendment, Congress should feel compelled to either recite those procedures in the convention call or leave such things to the Convention itself.

### (ii) Important Procedural Issues

The two most important issues concerning Convention Procedure are (i) the method of voting and (ii) the percentage required to propose an amendment. The original Ervin Bill provided that voting at the convention would be by state bloc, with each state afforded an equal voice.[520] At the original Constitutional Convention, with George Washington as President of the Convention, it was agreed that each state should have one vote.[521] Due to criticism of the state bloc method, the Ervin Bill was subsequently changed to provide for voting by individual delegate and also altering delegate apportionment to be based on representation in both the Senate and the House.[522]

Arch-liberal Professor Black thought that even this measure was "wholly indefensible" because it results in "over-representation of the less populous states"[523] which, by the way, is how both our Congress and our Electoral College are structured. In order for the suggested amendment to be proposed, it is important that voting be on a state bloc basis. If two-thirds of the states submit applications for a convention on a particular subject matter, it is likely that that same two-thirds will be able to reach an agreement as to the wording of the amendment and the vote for its proposal. The states in their memorials to Congress should request Congress to provide in its call that voting be by state bloc.

The second major issue concerning convention procedure is the percentage required to propose amendments. Should amendments be proposed by a simple majority or a two-thirds majority of the delegates to the convention? The Helms and Ervin Bills require a majority vote by the convention delegates to propose amendments.[524] Advocates of the two-thirds requirement noted that in Congress, where one house is checking another, a two-thirds vote is required to propose an amendment, so "it seems incredible" that Congress could not require a two-thirds majority for proposal of amendments by convention.[525]

"However, no argument satisfactorily dealt with the fact that article V expressly required a supermajority consensus for convention applications, ratifications, and the proposal of amendments by Congress, but does not require a supermajority vote for the proposal of amendments by a convention. Even more significantly, advocates of a two-thirds requirement ignored Congress' narrow role in the alternative amendment process. As noted above, any requirement imposed by Congress which is not necessary for Congress to bring a convention into existence or to choose the mode of ratification is outside Congress' constitutional authority. Since a convention, once underway, could itself decide what vote should be required to propose amendments, the two-thirds requirement predetermined by Congress would appear to be unconstitutional."[526]

In their memorial to Congress, the states should request Congress to establish a simple majority for proposing amendments, unless the convention votes for a higher percentage.

### (e) Mode of Ratification

Article V provides that, after the convention reports its proposals, Congress shall select the mode of ratification of the proposed amendment—ratification either by the legislatures of three-fourths of the states or by conventions in three-fourths of the states.[527] Congress has the sole discretion to decide upon the mode of ratification, so convention recommendations and state memorials to Congress in this regard can have no binding effect but can only act as persuasive measures. Ratification by legislatures, particularly the legislatures that have petitioned Congress for a convention, will be easier to achieve than ratification by state convention. Accordingly, states should request in their memorial that Congress set the mode of ratification to be by the legislatures of the states.

### (f) Ratification by the States

The sixth and final step is the ratification by the states. The major issue here is whether a state can rescind its ratification once it has ratified the amendment. When several state legislatures attempted to rescind their prior ratifications of the Equal Rights Amendment, the question of rescission became a hotly disputed issue.[528] The time limit on the amendment, however, expired before the courts could decide on this issue. Accordingly, it is yet unclear whether or not states can rescind.

## 3. Resolution and Memorial

In sum, in order to avoid real and congressionally or judicially contrived constitutional pitfalls that could impede the success of the alternate amendment process and still exercise as much influence over the process as possible, the state legislatures should submit an application to Congress that is relatively simple and straightforward, then submit a second document memorializing Congress to follow a certain course of action in regard to this call.

The following steps should be taken by the state legislatures in this regard:

1. To the fullest extent possible, all state legislatures should cause themselves to be in session on Wednesday, January 14, 1987, for the specific purpose of introducing a joint resolution and an accompanying memorial addressed to the Congress of the United States, on the subject of the fourteenth amendment.

2. Such joint resolutions should be adopted by the legislatures of the several states soon thereafter.

3. The following joint resolution and accompanying memorial dealing with proposed amendments to the United States Constitution should be adopted by every state legislature *without change* and in a uniform manner which will leave no question as to the intent of the several states.

A (JOINT) RESOLUTION* memorializing Congress to call a convention for the purpose of proposing amendments and considering an amendment to the Constitution of the United States relative to a repeal of the fourteenth and fifteenth articles of amendment.

Be It Resolved by the House of Representatives of the State of
_____ , the Senate concurring, that this Legislature does hereby respectfully make application to the Congress of the United States to call a convention for the purpose of proposing amendments, and in particular, considering the following article as an amendment to the Constitution of the United States, to wit:

---

*This resolution should be in whatever technical form the state employs for a single resolution of both houses of the legislature which does not require the Governor to approve or veto.

## ARTICLE OF AMENDMENT XXVII

Section 1.

The fourteenth and fifteenth articles of amendment to the Constitution of the United States are hereby repealed. Further, in order to halt the encroachment into the reserved powers of the states by the United States and its judicial branch, the tenth article of amendment is hereby amended to read as follows:

The powers not expressly delegated to the United States by the Constitution, nor prohibited by it to the States, are reserved to the States respectively, or to the people.

Section 2.

No person shall be a citizen of the United States unless he is a non-Hispanic white of the European race, in whom there is no ascertainable trace of Negro blood, nor more than one-eighth Mongolian, Asian, Asia Minor, Middle Eastern, Semitic, Near Eastern, American Indian, Malay or other non-European or nonwhite blood, provided that Hispanic whites, defined as anyone with an Hispanic ancestor, may be citizens if, in addition to meeting the aforesaid ascertainable trace and percentage tests, they are in appearance indistinguishable from Americans whose ancestral home is the British Isles or Northwestern Europe. Only citizens shall have the right and privilege to reside permanently in the United States.

Section 3.

The Congress and the several states, except where expressly preempted by the Congress, shall have concurrent power to enforce the provisions of this article by appropriate legislation, in coordination with the President, as such legislation concerns the making of treaties pursuant to Article 2, Section 2 of the Constitution.

Be It Further Resolved that if Congress shall have proposed an amendment to the Constitution identical with that contained in this resolution prior to January 1, 1989, this application for a convention shall no longer be of any force or effect.

Be it Further Resolved that a duly attested copy of this resolution be immediately transmitted to the Secretary of the State of the United States, the Clerk of the House of Representatives of the United States and to each member of the Congress from this State.

The memorial to Congress to accompany the applications by the state legislatures to call a convention should be as follows:

A (JOINT) RESOLUTION* memorializing Congress to take certain action pursuant to its duty under Article V to call a convention when the requisite number of states have submitted applications therefor.

WHEREAS, the House of Representatives of this State, with the Senate concurring, made application to the Congress of the United States to call a convention for the purpose of proposing amendments, and, in particular, considering an amendment to the Constitution of the United States relative to a repeal of the fourteenth and fifteenth articles of amendment; and

WHEREAS, once two-thirds of the several states have submitted contemporaneous applications to call a convention relative to the same subject matter, Congress is bound by Article V of the Constitution to call a convention; and

WHEREAS, Article V does not prescribe the procedural details for calling a convention. It also gives no indication of how a convention would be run, nor does it assign responsibility for this determination. There has never been a convention called under Article V and there are virtually no precedents to follow; and

WHEREAS, Congress may have, within limitations, the constitutional powers to prescribe the procedural details for calling a convention, but may or may not have the constitutional power to prescribe the procedure of the convention itself; and

WHEREAS, it is felt that Congress will be unsure as to the procedural details it should adopt relative to the calling of a convention and to what extent it should attempt to regulate the convention procedure; and

---

*This resolution should be in whatever technical form the state employs for a single resolution of both houses of the legislature which does not require the Governor to approve or veto.

WHEREAS, it is feared that Congress might abuse its powers over the calling of a convention and the lack of precedents and place undue restrictions on the convention process, including the procedural details for calling the convention and the procedures of the convention itself that would allow Congress to obstruct the proposing of an amendment relative to the repeal of the fourteenth and fifteenth articles of amendment; and

WHEREAS, this State is desirous of setting forth in clear and unmistakable terms the procedural details that it hopes Congress will follow in calling the convention, and the action or inaction, it hopes Congress will take in regard to the procedure of the convention itself.

NOW THEREFORE BE IT RESOLVED by the House of Representatives of the State of _____, the Senate concurring, that the Congress of the United States be earnestly requested to adopt and prescribe the following procedure in calling the convention:

1. The application concerning an amendment to the Constitution of the United States relative to a repeal of the fourteenth and fifteenth articles of amendment, shall remain effective for seven calendar years after the date it is received by the Congress.

2. The Vice President of the United States shall preside over the convention until the convention elects a presiding officer.

3. The President of the United States shall have no veto power over the convention process.

4. The governors of the states shall have no veto power over the applications to call a convention.

5. Each state shall send three delegates to the convention.

6. Voting at the convention shall be by state bloc.

7. Congress shall make no restrictions regarding the subject matter of the convention.

8. Amendments shall be proposed by simple majority unless the convention delegates elect otherwise. States shall appoint delegates in a manner as the legislatures thereof may direct.

9. Congress shall call for the convention within three months of the day it receives applications from the requisite number of states.

10. Congress shall cause the convention to be held within six months from the date of the call of the convention in Washington, D. C.

11. Upon proposal of any amendment through the convention, Congress shall designate ratification thereof by the legislatures of three fourths of the Several States within seven years of its submission.

BE IT FURTHER RESOLVED that a duly attested copy of this resolution be immediately transmitted to the Secretary of State of the United States, the Clerk of the House of Representatives of the United States and to each member of the Congress from this state.

# VIII. CONCLUSION

It is hoped that the legislatures of the several states, and the people also, will scrutinize this amendment in order to determine what action should be taken to either further its progress towards proposal and ratification or to thwart and defeat it. In any event, regardless of the action, or inaction, taken by this generation, the concepts embraced by this amendment will never totally disappear. There will always be some who favor them and some who will oppose them.

If this amendment does not fall into the obscurity of most printed pages, but comes before the public at large, then most likely the public consciousness will be stirred. At the outset, the opposition will be larger than the support, but because of the polemic nature of the concepts set forth herein, the indifferent will probably be few. At first, the media will rail against the amendment and intimidate many supporters from speaking out. Still, perhaps enough of America and her state legislators will unite to take decisive action for ratification. It is feared, however, that many opponents will not think deeply about the amendment, but only reject it as a conditioned response to the media's campaign. It is hoped that serious consideration of the amendment will be given by all, and that each person will make a conscious and deliberate decision one way or the other and act accordingly. If deep thought is given by the population, I am confident that the bulk of the nation will support the amendment. Then the true will of the American people can be manifest and her destiny can be set, not by conditioned responses or social ignorance, but by thinking men concerned for the land, heritage and principles that have given them so much bounty. The time to act is now.

# POSTSCRIPT

Those of you who favor the concepts embraced by this amendment are urged to support its proposal and ratification by sending (1) a copy of this text to your state legislator with a letter of support and (2) your contributions to:

League of Pace Amendment Advocates
P. O. Box 711207
Los Angeles, California 90071

# NOTES

1. R. REAGAN, RENDEZVOUS WITH DESTINY 9 (1981).

2. During America's turbulent years, the mid-sixties through the mid-seventies, the violence and dissension in the streets, in the schools and on the campuses were, for the most part, attributable to the young. "The hippies, yippies, activists, strikers, paraders, hijackers and other malcontents manifesting displeasure with the established order [were], with very few exceptions, in the first half of their life span." Hendry, *Ethics, Values and the Common Good as Guidelines for a World Community,* 7 Ottawa L. Rev. 330, 331 (1975). Many of these persons whose actions were outrageous while young will be outraged now at the recommendations of this text. During this same period and before, the presence of Negroes and other coloreds within the white society was often controversial and provoked violence. For example, in the Southern Manifesto, 19 Senators and 77 Congressmen protested racial integration. (102 Cong. Rec., No. 43, pp. 3948, 4004, March 12, 1956). And in 1957, the President sent federal troops to Arkansas to force integration. Many of these people whose presence within white society in 1957 caused outrage will also be outraged.

3. R. REAGAN, *supra* note 1, at 25.

4. "It must be emphasized that *social* scientific research has fallen behind that in the physical sciences. We do not know the effect of the eradication of slums on the general welfare of the slum's inmates. We do not know how far welfare programs assist in the common good. Do they perpetuate idleness? Do the "hand-outs" go to the ones in need? We do not know the effect of a guaranteed annual wage. Will it make for stagnant, shiftless and irresponsible individuals and social groups?" Hendry, *supra* note 2, at 358.

5. *See* NEWSWEEK, Feb. 27, 1984, at 49.

6. Los Angeles Times, Apr. 16, 1984, Sec. I, at 6, col. 3.

7. U.S. DEPARTMENT OF COMMERCE, BUREAU OF THE CENSUS, HISTORICAL STATISTICS OF THE UNITED STATES, COLONIAL TIMES TO 1970, 57 (1975). [hereinafter cited as HISTORICAL STATISTICS].

8. *Id.* at 45.

9. *See, e.g.*, U.S. DEPARTMENT OF COMMERCE, BUREAU OF THE CENSUS, MONEY INCOME AND POVERTY STATUS OF FAMILIES AND PERSONS IN THE U.S.: 1982, (Advance Data from the March 1983 Current Population Survey), 2.

10. In the *Enumerators' Reference Manual*, Item 9, 1950 Census, the following directions are given in regard to racial classification: "115. *Mexicans*—Report 'White' (W) for Mexicans unless they are definitely of Indian or other nonwhite race." 3 Race Relations L. Rep. 588 (1958).

11. *See, e.g.*, employment questionnaires given by California state colleges and universities to prospective professors and lecturers or other equal opportunity employers.

12. HISTORICAL STATISTICS, *supra* note 7, at 9.

13.. *Id.*

14. *See* note 10.

15. NEWSWEEK, Jan. 17, 1983, at 23.

16. *Id.*

17. NEWSPAPER ENTERPRISES ASSOCIATION, INC., THE WORLD ALMANAC & BOOK OF FACTS, 210 (1983).

18. NEWSWEEK, Jan. 17, 1983, at 22.

19. Los Angeles Times, Apr. 1, 1984, Sec. I, at 1, col. 1.

20. NEWSWEEK, Jan. 17, 1983, at 22, 23.

21. *Id.*

22. HISTORICAL STATISTICS *supra* note 7, at 105, 107, 109.

23. Los Angeles Daily News, May 9, 1984, (News) at 1 cols. 3-4. The fertility rate for blacks in America is 85 per 1000.

24. Los Angeles Times, Apr. 16, 1984, Sec. I, at 6, col. 3.

25. HISTORICAL STATISTICS, *supra* note 7 at 45.

26. *Id.*

27. NEWSWEEK, Jan. 17, 1983 at 24.

28. *Id.* at 25.

29. HISTORICAL STATISTICS, *supra* note 7 at 25.

30. *Id.*

31. NEWSWEEK, Jan. 17, 1983, at 25.

32. *Id*. Currently, more than one-fourth of all families with children have only one parent present. Los Angeles Herald, May 14, 1985, Sec. A, at 1, col. 4.

33. R. and D. Roy, *Is Monogamy Outdated?* in THE NEW SEXUAL REVOLUTION 131 (L. Kirkendall and N. Whitehurst ed. 1971). [hereinafter cited as NEW SEXUAL REVOLUTION].

34. *Id*.

35. NEWSWEEK, Jan. 17, 1983, at 21. The following table from 26 CHRISTIANITY TODAY 41 (Mar. 19, 1982) demonstrates the trend in recent years toward promiscuity in our teenage girls:

## PERCENTAGE OF NEVER MARRIED WOMEN ENGAGING IN SEX

| Age | 1971 | 1976 | 1979 | Percent Increase 1971-79 |
|-----|------|------|------|--------------------------|
| 15 | 14.4 | 18.6 | 22.5 | 56.2 |
| 16 | 20.9 | 28.9 | 37.8 | 80.9 |
| 17 | 26.1 | 42.9 | 48.5 | 85.5 |
| 18 | 39.7 | 51.4 | 56.9 | 43.3 |
| 19 | 46.4 | 59.5 | 69 | 48.7 |

SOURCE: Melvin Zelnik and John F. Kantner, "Sexual Activity, Contraceptive Use and Pregnancy among Metropolitan Area Teenagers, 1971-1979"; Family Planning Perspectives, Vol. 12, no. 5, Sept.-Oct. 1980

36. NEWSWEEK, Jan. 17, 1983 at 25.

37. *Id.*

38. TIME, Apr. 9, 1984, at 76.

39. *Id.*

40. Los Angeles Daily News, July 19, 1984, (News) at 1, cols.3-6. This source said that unmarried couples living together "more than tripled." Other sources, however, said that the increase was "four-fold," *see* text at note 28.

41. Willemsen, *Justice Tobriner and the Tolerance of Evolving Lifestyles: Adapting the Law to Social Change*, 29 Hastings L.J. 73, 74 (1977).

42. Los Angeles Daily News, July 19, 1984, (News) at 1, col. 4.

43. TIME, Apr. 9, 1984, at 77.

44. AMBASSADOR COLLEGE, THE SILENT EPIDEMIC 4 (1977).

45. TIME, Feb. 4, 1985, at 67.

46. *Id.*

47. *Id.*

48. AMBASSADOR COLLEGE, THE SILENT EPIDEMIC 4 (1977); TIME, Feb. 4, 1985, at 67.

49. Buchanan, *AIDS Soon Will Kill More Americans than Viet War Did*, Los Angeles Daily News, Nov. 14, 1984 (U.S./World) at 7, col. 5. Because the vectors are so promiscuous the destructive potential of the disease is as great as the Black Death which devastated Europe in the 14th Century.

50. 1 Am. Jur. 2d, *Abortion*, Sec. 1.5 (pocket part, 1984).

51. 410 U.S. 113 (1973).

52. THE WORLD ALMANAC & BOOK OF FACTS, *supra* note 17 at 961.

53. Los Angeles Daily News, Jl. 11, 1984, (News) at 1, col. 4.

54. C. JUDGE, THE BOOK OF AMERICAN RANKINGS 42 (1979).

55. Los Angeles Times, Jan. 1, 1984, Sec. I, at 1 col. 1.

56. 70 Am. Jur. 2d *Sodomy*, Sec. 25 (1973). *See also, ex parte Miller* 23 Idaho 403, 129 P. 1075.

57. "In the 'gay dark ages' before the sexual revolution of the 1960s and '70s, most homosexuals led separate public and private lives, fearful of losing their jobs or their families' love. All fifty states had laws against homosexual relations and gays were often arrested." Los Angeles Times, Jan. 1, 1984 Sec. I, at 32, col. 1.

58. *Id*.

59. Los Angeles Daily News, Apr. 30, 1984, (L.A. Life) at 17, col. 1.

60. Los Angeles Times, January 1, 1984, Sec. I, at 7, col. 1.

61. A Riverside, California homosexual, David Frater, recently adopted a son and "has plans to adopt more wards of the court." Id.

62. *Commonwealth v. Bonadio* [1980, Pa.] 415 A. 2d 47.

63. 42 ALR Fed. 189, 192 .

64. 1973, DC Cal 6 CCH EPD par. 8934.

65. 42 ALR Fed. 189, 193.

66. 1973 DC Md. 359 F Supp 843, aff. on other grounds, CA 4 Md. 491 Fed 498, cert. den 419 US 836, 42 L Ed 63, 95 S.Ct. 64.

67. Los Angeles Times, June 29, 1984, Sec. I, at 2, col. 3.

68. *T. v. T.* 140 N.J. Super. 77, 355 A. 2d 204, 63 ALR 3rd 68. (pocket part, 1984).

69. U.S. DEPARTMENT OF COMMERCE, SOCIAL INDICATORS III, at 515 (1980); AMERICAN INSTITUTE OF PUBLIC OPINION, THE GALLUP POLL: PUBLIC OPINION, 1972-199, THE GALLUP OPINION INDEX, rep. no. 145 (1978).

70. *Id*.

71. U.S. DEPARTMENT OF COMMERCE, SOCIAL INDICATORS III, at 515 (1980); NATIONAL OPINION RESEARCH CENTER, UNIVERSITY OF CHICAGO, NATIONAL DATA PROGRAM FOR THE SOCIAL SCIENCES, GENERAL SOCIAL SURVEYS, 1972-1978: CUMULATIVE CODEBOOK.

72. *Id*.

73. *Engel v. Vitale* 370 U.S. 421 (1962); *Abington Township School Dist. v. Schempp* 374 U.S. 203 (1963).

74. reprinted in Am. Jur. 2d, Desk Book, Item No. 183, at 746 (1979).

75. L.S. Tao, *Crime, Punishment and Law Enforcement*, 23 Wayne L. Rev. 1395, 1398 (1977).

76. HISTORICAL STATISTICS, *supra* note 7, at 413.

77. A J 2d, Desk Book, Item No. 77, at 129 (1979).

78. Los Angeles Daily News, June 10, 1984, (U.S./News) at 1, col. 3.

79. *Id*.

80. *Id.*

81. S. JANUS, THE DEATH OF INNOCENCE 16 (1981).

82. FACTS ON FILE, CURRENT AFFAIRS ATLAS 126 (D. Paneth, ed. 1979).

83. Los Angeles Times, Jan. 8, 1984, Sec. I, at 20, col. 1.

84. *Id.*

85. Los Angeles Daily News, Sept. 8, 1984, (News) at 1, cols. 1-3.

86. C. J. CALMAN, THE MORMON TABERNACLE CHOIR 99 (1979).

87. A casual review of *Billboard*, August 25, 1984, a newsweekly of music and entertainment contains full page spreads of tattooed, leather and metal groups such as "Wasp" and Mohawk-coiffured and spike-haired groups such as "Thompson Twins," in addition to "Boy George and the Culture Club."

88. Los Angeles Daily News, Sept. 8, 1984 (News) at 12, col. 5.

89. *See* Los Angeles Daily News, April 30, 1984, (L.A. Life) at 17, col. 1; Los Angeles Daily News, Sept. 14, 1984 (L.A. Life) at 26, col. 1; Los Angeles Times, Jan. 1, 1984, Sec. I, at 3, col. 3.

90. NEWSPAPER ENTERPRISE ASSOCIATION, INC., THE WORLD ALMANAC & BOOK OF FACTS 210 (1983).

91. *Id.*

92. Salt Lake City Deseret News, Mar. 25, 1984 (Church News) at 16, col. 2.

93. As an illustration of how far we have come, in the 1952-1955 volume of the Index to Legal Periodicals, there are 14 articles regarding obscenity over a three-year span. In the 1982-1983 volume there were 28 articles over a one-year span. Where the 1952-1955 articles dealt with issues like obscene postcards, 1984 articles "grapple" with the constitutionality of kiddie porn.

94. PEOPLE, Jl. 16, 1984, at 32.

95. For example, a "Dynasty" script calls for a homosexual character to kiss his male partner on screen. PEOPLE, Nov. 26, 1984, at 41.

96. Los Angeles Times, Feb. 12, 1984, Sec.I, at 1, col.1.

97. *Id.*

98. *Id.*

99. The suit was brought in small claims court in Indianapolis by a father who wanted to teach his child how to sue. Information obtained in a telephone conversation with Borden, Inc., attorney, Jerome R. Schindler (Jan. 8, 1985).

100. Margolick, *Cravath Measures the Price of Victory in Long IBM Case*, Los Angeles Daily J., Jan. 26, 1982, at 7, col. 1.

101. Los Angeles Daily News, June 29, 1984, (News) at 9, col. 4.

102. Am. Jur. 2d, Desk Book, Item No. 66, at 111 (pocket part, 1984).

103. *Id*.

104. Los Angeles Times, Feb. 19, 1984, Sec. I, at 8, col. 1; Feb. 18, 1984, Sec. I, at 8, cols. 3-5; Feb. 12, 1984, Sec. I, at 1, col. 1.

105. Los Angeles Times, Feb. 12, 1984, Sec. I, at 18, col. 1.

106. MONEY INCOME AND POVERTY STATUS OF FAMILIES AND PERSONS IN THE U.S.: 1982, *supra* note 9, at 21.

107. *Id*.

108. *Id*.

109. Los Angeles Times, Mar. 11, 1984, Sec. I, at 2, col. 1.

110. MONEY INCOME AND POVERTY STATUS OF FAMILIES AND PERSONS IN THE U.S.: 1982, *supra* note 9, at 21.

111. U.S. NEWS & WORLD REPORT, Dec. 24, 1984 at 39.

112. *Id*.

113. *Id*.

114. MONEY INCOME AND POVERTY STATUS OF FAMILIES AND PERSONS IN THE U.S.: 1982, *supra* note 9, at 21.

115. *Id*.

116. *Id*.

117. *Id*.

118. NEWSPAPER ENTERPRISE ASSOCIATION, INC., THE WORLD ALMANAC & BOOK OF FACTS 1983, at 575.

119. *Grading Time for U.S. Schools*, SCHOLASTIC UPDATE, Feb. 3, 1984, at 2.

120. *Id*. at 3.

121. H. Giroux, *Public Philosophy and the Crisis in Education,* 54 Harv. Educ. Rev. 187 (May 1984); USA Today, May 13, 1985, Sec. A, at 9, col. 6.

122. EDUCATIONAL TESTING SERVICE, COLLEGE-BOUND SENIORS, 1983, at 4 (1983). Information for 1963 was obtained through a telephone conversation with the Educational Testing Service.

123. SCHOLASTIC UPDATE, *supra* note 119.

124. H. Giroux, *supra* note 121, at 189.

125. Los Angeles Daily News, May 27, 1984, (News) at 6, col. 1.

126. SCHOLASTIC UPDATE, *supra* note 119, at 3.

127. The following table was quoted on page J-4 in the 1983 edition of *Japanese Technology Today,* a magazine advertisement supplement sponsored by Japanese Corporations and written by Dr. James C. Abegglen and Akio Etori:

| SHARE OF WORLD GNP 1960-1980 | | |
| --- | --- | --- |
| | 1960 | 1970 | 1980 |
| US | 33.7% | 30.2% | 21.5% |
| EEC | 17.5 | 19.3 | 22.4 |
| Japan | 2.9 | 6.0 | 9.0 |
| USSR | 15.2 | 15.9 | 11.6 |
| PRC | 4.4 | 4.9 | 4.7 |
| Other | 26.3 | 23.7 | 30.8 |
| Total | 100.0 | 100.0 | 100.0 |

Source: 2000 Nen No Nihon (Japan in the Year 2000), Keizai Kikaku Cho Sogo Keikaku Kyoku Hen, Nihon Keizai Shimbunsha, Tokyo, 1982, p. 31.

128. *Japan Technology Today, Id.*

129. Los Angeles Times, March 1, 1985, Sec. IV, at 1, Col. 1

130. W. Wishard, *Productivity and American World Competitiveness*, 48 VITAL SPEECHES OF THE DAY 316 (Mar. 1, 1982).

131. T. Warren, *Warning to America*, 50 VITAL SPEECHES OF THE DAY 147 (Dec. 15, 1983).

132. MOTOR VEHICLE MANUFACTURER'S ASSOCIATION OF THE UNITED STATES, WORLD MOTOR VEHICLE DATA 10 (1982).

133. *Id.*

134. *Id.*

135. *Id.*

136. FAIRCHILD PUBLICATIONS, INC., METAL STATISTICS 1983 AMERICAN METAL MARKET 163-164 (1983).

137. *Id.*

138. *Id.*

139. CURRENT AFFAIRS ATLAS, *supra* note 82, at 35.

140. *Id.*

141. *Id.*

142. *Id.*

143. *Id.*

144. U.S. DEPARTMENT OF COMMERCE, BUREAU OF INDUSTRIAL ECONOMICS, 1984 U.S. INDUSTRIAL OUTLOOK 33-1 (1984).

145. *Id.* at 33-2.

146. *Id.*

147. *Id.*

148. Los Angeles Times, Mar. 23, 1984, Sec. IV, at 1, col. 2.

149. *Id.*

150. U.S. DEPARTMENT OF COMMERCE, THE U.S. INDUSTRIAL OUTLOOK FOR 1961 at 164 (1961).

151. 1984 U.S. INDUSTRIAL OUTLOOK, *supra* note 144, at 143-6.

152 THE U.S. INDUSTRIAL OUTLOOK FOR 1961, *supra* note 150.

153. U.S. DEPARTMENT OF COMMERCE, THE U.S. INDUSTRIAL OUTLOOK FOR 1977 at 325 (1977).

154. 1984 U.S. INDUSTRIAL OUTLOOK, *supra* note 144, at 143-6.

155. *Id.*

156. *Id.*

157. *Id.*

158. *Id.* at 27-3.

159. *Id.* at 37-2.

160. *Id.* at 44-14.

161. W. Wilshard, *supra* note 130, at 317.

162. *Id.*

163. NEWSWEEK, Aug. 2, 1982, at 12.

164. *Id.*

165. *Id.*

166. *Id.*; TIME, Apr. 27, 1981, at 47.

167. NEWSWEEK, Aug. 2, 1982, at 12.

168. *Id.* at 15.

169. U.S. Const. preamble.

170. *See*: Webster's New World Dictionary, 2d ed. *s.v.* "ruin," "fall."

171. *Id.*

172. Certain scholars claim that the poorer educational performance by nonwhites in general is due, in part, to genetics. *See* Jensen, *How Much Can We Boost IQ and Scolastic Achievement?*, 39 Harv. Educ. Rev. 1 (1969).

173. According to the House of Representatives' Select Committee on Children, Youth and Families, one out of five children and one out of two black children in America live in poverty-stricken families. Los Angeles Times, March 11, 1984, Sec. I, at 2, col. 1.

174. Not only do blacks have a higher crime rate than whites, black criminal defendants are more likely to receive a more severe sentence than whites. This is due, in part, because black criminal defendants are more likely to have a serious charge or prior criminal record than their white counterparts. Spohn, Gruhl and Welch, *The Effects of Race on Sentencing: a Re-examination of an Unsettled Question* 16 Law and Society Rev. 71, 72 (1981-82).

175. "As an average, black infants die at a rate twice that of white infants. In some cities, black babies are dying at a rate almost four times the white mortality rate. The gap between white and black infant deaths is widening. Black infant mortality rates—which were 86 percent higher than white rates— were 95 percent higher that white rates by 1982." Food Research and Action Center, *Black and White Infant Deaths: a Widening Gap*, 18 Clearinghouse Review 260 (July 1984).

176. Recent immigrants from Haiti, Indochina and Cuba, for example, have brought with them a much higher incidence of AIDS, leprosy and mental disorders than is found in the general public.

177. Government regulations regarding race and employment, such as equal opportunity employment policies, affirmative action, etc., cause decreases in productivity not only because of the increase in counterproductive regulations arising therefrom, but also because employers are no longer able to base hiring needs on their own standards for success without fear of civil rights reprisals.

178. *See* Note 23 and accompanying text.

179. According to the Bureau of the Census, the younger generation reported having a higher percentage of multiracial ancestry than their elders. NEWSWEEK, Jan. 17, 1983 at 22; *see also*: *Numbers Increase on Interracial Marriage* 66 JET 26 (Jl. 30, 1984).

180. For example, when the Southern states first opposed integration of the schools in 1965 by asserting the doctrine of interposition, which the U.S. Supreme Court later ruled unconstitutional, California adopted an anti-interposition memorial to Congress stating that the South's acts were "based solely upon bigotry and race prejudice" and "are repugnant to every moral, religious and political principle of our great American democracy." House Resolution no. 16 of the California Legislature, passed March 15, 1956.

181. GABRIELLE BROWN, THE NEW CELIBACY (1980).

182. *See, e.g.*, Evans and Novak, *State of Race Relations in Deep South Seems Polarized Again*, Los Angeles Daily News, Sept. 29, 1984 (U.S./ World) at 7, col. 1; "Studies often show that with integration there is less interracial acceptance and more prejudice." Halliman, *Classroom Racial Composition and Children's Friendships*, 61 (no.1) Social Forces 56, 57 (Sept. 1982). Further, "[i]t is generally known that students prefer members of their own race as friends than members of another race." *Id.* at 58. And, [t]he tolerance of residential integration among whites varied depending upon the level of integration. Willingness to live next door to a black family always exceeded willingness to live among large numbers of blacks." Smith, *Attitudes of Whites Toward Residential Integration*, 43 Phylon 368, 377 (Winter 1982).

183. This slogan was used in a U.S. military poster campaign in Seoul, Korea, in May 1983 in an effort to elevate the standards of conduct of the troops.

184. U.S. Const. amend. XVIII.

185. 24 Am Jur 2d, *Divorce and Separation*, generally Secs. 514- 771 (1983).

186. Granelli, *Meet Mr. Palimony: Marvin Michelson's Practice for the Stars*, Nat'l. L. J., Oct. 11, 1982 at 1 col. 2.

187. In addition to laws relating to child custody, there are laws regarding child snatching (Federal Parental Kidnapping Act of 1980), grandparents' visitation rights (3 Am J. Trial Advocacy 589-591 (1980), and visitation rights for homosexual parents (*J.L.P.v. D.f.P.* 643 S.W. 2d 865 (Mo. App. 1982).

188. Further, the state of today's society makes it necessary for the courts to grapple with parents' morals and child custody (Roberts, *'Twas Brillig and the Court did Gyre, Gimble and Outgrabe (parents morals and child custody)*, 69 Ill. B. J. 154 (1980).

189. *See, e.g.*, Los Angeles Daily News, June 21, 1984 (News) at 18, col. 1, where a judge in Santa Ana awarded joint custody of a cockapoo to a divorced couple who continued their custody battle beyond normal limits for custody disputes involving children.

190. *Hair v. Hair* 31 S.C. Eq. 163, 174 (1858).

191. *Scrogins v. Scrogins* 14 N.C. 535, 542 (1832).

192. Note, *Early Statutory and Common Law of Divorce in North Carolina*, 41 N.C. L. Rev. 604 (1963).

193. POYNTER, MARRIAGE & DIVORCE 168 (1836), *cited in Id.* at 609.

194. McNamara, *Should Divorce Be Made Respectable?*, 41 Chi. Bar Rec. 84 (1959).

195. Sayre, *Divorce for the Unworthy*, 18 Law & Contemp. Prob. 26, 27 (1953).

196. McNamara, *supra* note 194 at 85.

197. Silbert, *Random Thoughts on Marriage and Divorce*, 4 Clev.-Mar. L. Rev. 91, 94 (1955).

198. *Id.* at 93.

199. Fenberg, *Can Divorce Be Made Respectable?*, 40 Chi. Bar Rec. 424 (1959), *cited in* 41 Chi. Bar Rec. 84 (1959).

200. MAGRUDER, AMERICAN GOVERNMENT IN 1921, title page (1921).

201. Webster's New World Dictionary, 2d ed., *s.v* "morality."

202. Sagarin, *On Obscenity and Pornography* in NEW SEXUAL REVOLUTION, *supra* note 33 at 106.

203. *Id.*

204. *See, e.g.*, EDMUND WILSON, MEMOIRS OF HECATE COUNTY, *cited in Id.*

205. New York Times, Apr. 10, 1969, *cited in* Sagarin, *supra* note 202.

206. 410 U.S. 113 (1973).

207. R. GUYON, SEX LIFE AND SEX ETHICS 309-310 (1933) *cited in* Seal, *Cross-Cultral Sexual Practices*, in NEW SEXUAL REVOLUTION, *supra* note 33 at 21.

208. Seal, *Id*. at 21.

209. Pohlman, *Contraception In and Out of Marriage* in NEW SEXUAL REVOLUTION, *supra* note 33 at 191.

210. Ellis, *A Rational Sexual Morality*, in NEW SEXUAL REVOLUTION, *supra* note 33 at 59.

211. *Doe v. Doe* 222 Va. 763 at 748; 284 S.E. 2d 799, 806 (1981); *See also* Comment, *Doe v. Doe: Destroying the Presumption that Homosexual Parents are Unfit— The New Burden of Proof*, 16 U. of Rich. L. Rev. 851.

212. Roy, *supra* note 33 at 143.

213. *Id*. at 134.

214. Sagarin, *supra* note 202 at 111.

215. Ellis, *supra* note 210 at 55.

216 *Id*. at 53-54.

217. Kurtz, *Preface: Humanism and the Sexual Revolution*, in NEW SEXUAL REVOLUTION, *supra* note 33, at x.

218. 26 CHRISTIANITY TODAY, Mar. 19, 1982 at 58.

219. *Id*. at 41.

220. *Id*.

221. Densen-Gerber, *Introduction* in JANUS *supra* note 81 at 10.

222. *Id*.

223. *Id*.

224. *Id*. at 12.

225. Ohlson, *Adultery: A Review*, 17 B.U.L.Rev. 328, 353 (1937).

226. Seal, *supra* note 207 at 21-22.

227. WILLIAM N. STEPHENS, THE FAMILY IN CROSS-CULTURAL PERSPECTIVE 265 (1963); Seal, *supra* note 207 at 27.

228. Howard, *Margaret Mead, 'Self-appointed Mater Familias to the World'*, Simthsonian, Sept. 1984 at 118.

229. ALFRED C. KINSEY, WARDELL B. POMEROW, CLYDE E. MARTIN, PAUL H. GEBBARD, SEXUAL BEHAVIOR IN THE HUMAN FEMALE 413 (1953), *cited in* Seal, *supra* note 207 at 24.

230. Whitehurst, *American Sexophobia*, NEW SEXUAL REVOLUTION, *supra* note 33 at 12.

231. Ellis, *supra* note 210 at 56.

232. *Id*. at 53.

233. On the death of my ninth great-grandfather, Captain Johnson, in Roxbury, Massachusetts, in 1659, and my eighth great-grandfather, Captain Issac Johnson, in Roxbury, Massachusetts, in 1673, their "beloved" wives received the bulk of their estates and were appointed "sole executrix" of the wills of their husbands. This is hardly an example of women being "property." PAUL FRANKLIN JOHNSON, GENEALOGY OF CAPTAIN JOHN JOHNSON 418, 422 (1951).

234. Ohlson, *Adultery: A Review*, 17 B. U. L. Rev. 328, 349-352 (1957).

235. *Id*. at 354-368.

236. ST. THOMAS AQUINAS, ON THE GOVERNANCE OF RULERS 33 (G. Phelan trans. 1938).

237. *See: Religion, Philosophy of*, 15 ENCYCLOPAEDIA BRITANNICA 592-596 (1974).

238. *Id*. at 596.

239. Mayflower Compact, *reprinted in* Am. Jur. 2d. Desk Book, Item no. 183 (1984).

240. Maryland Toleration Act, *reprinted in* Am. Jur. 2d. Desk Book, Item no. 184 (1984).

241. Virginia Bill of Rights, *reprinted in* Am. Jur. 2d. Desk Book, Item no. 185 (1984).

242. Massachusetts Bill of Rights of 1780, *reprinted in* Am. Jur. 2d. Desk Book, Item no. 188 (1984).

243. U.S. Const. preamble.

244. Department of State Bulletin, April 1984 at 15.

245. *See infra* notes 258 and 259 and accompanying text.

246. *See*: Farris, *My Client is the Moral Majority*, 9 Barrister no. 2 (Spring 1982) at 12, 14.

247. In 1962, nondenominational prayers were prohibited. *Engel v. Vitale* 370 U.S. 421 (1962). In 1963, Bible reading was banned. *Hoington Township School Dist. v. Schempp* 374 U.S. 203 (1963). In that case, a Pennsylvania statute required that "at least ten verses from the Holy Bible shall be read, without comment, at the opening of each public school on each school day. Any child shall be excused from such Bible reading, or attending such Bible reading, upon the written request of his parent or guardian." 24 PA Cons. Stat. Sec. 15-1516 (Purdon Supp. 1960).

248. 370 U.S. 421 (1962).

249. 374 U.S. 203 (1963).

250. 343 U.S. 306 (1952).

251. 36 ALR 3d. 1256-1273.

252. *Board of Education v. Minor* 23 Ohio St. 211 (Ohio 1872).

253. *State v. Mockus* 120 Me 84, 113 A 39 (Maine 1921).

254. *Id.*

255. Hitchcock, *The Supreme Court and Religion: Historical Overview and Future Prognosis*, 24 St. Louis U. L. J. 185 (1980).

256. *Id.* at 200.

257. *Id.* at 193.

258. *Id.* at 201.

259. *Id.* at 198.

260. Zimring & Hawkins, *Ideology and Euphoria in Crime Control*, 10 U. Tol. L. Rev. 370 (1979).

261. *Id.*

262. *President's Radio Address on Law Enforcement and Drug Abuse Prevention*, 9 Weekly Comp. of Pres. Doc. 246 (Mar. 10, 1973).

263. E. VAN DEN HAAG, PUNISHING CRIMINALS 264 (1965).

264. Martinson, Letter to the Editor on Theories of Crime, COMMENTARY, Oct. 1974 at 12, *cited in* Zimring & Hawkins, *supra* note 260 at 373.

265. Zimring & Hawkins, *supra* note 260 at 374.

266. J. WILSON, THINKING ABOUT CRIME 209 (1975).

267. Zimring & Hawkins, *supra* note 260 at 381.

268. J. EDGAR HOOVER, STATEMENTS IN FAVOR OF THE DEATH PENALTY IN AMERICA 134 (1964).

269. P. TAPPER, CRIME, JUSTICE AND CORRECTION 245-46 (1960).

270. FACTS ON FILE, CRIME AND PUNISHMENT IN AMERICA 8 (J. Buncher, ed., 1978) [*hereinafter cited as* CRIME AND PUNISHMENT].

271. *Id.*

272. *Id.*

273. 367 U.S. 643 (1961).

274. CRIME AND PUNISHMENT, *supra* note 270 at 89.

275. For example, see statements of Chief Justice Warren Burger in *Id.*

276. 384 U.S. 486 (1966).

277. CRIME AND PUNISHMENT, *supra* note 270 at 89-90.

278. *See, e.g., Michigan v. Tucker* 417 U.S. 422 (1974) and *Oregon v. Mathieson* 429 U.S. 492 (1977).

279. *Castenada v. Partida* 430 U.S. 482 (1977).

280. 408 U.S. 258 (1972).

281. CRIME AND PUNISHMENT, *supra* note 270 at 207.

282. *Rhem v. Malcolm* 371 F. Supp. 594 (S.D.N.Y. 1974) *aff'd* 507 F.2d. 333 (2d Cir. 1974).

283. CRIME AND PUNISHMENT, *supra* note 270 at 259.

284. *Bounds v. Smith* 430 U.S. 817 (1977).

285. 418 U.S. 539 (1974).

286. J. FINNIS, NATURAL LAW AND NATURAL RIGHTS 260 (1980).

287. Tao, *Crime, Punishment and Law Enforcement*, 23 Wayne L. Rev. 1357, 1412 (1977).

288. READERS DIGEST, July 1984, inside front cover.

289. *Paris Adult Theatre I v. Slaton* 413 U.S. 49 (1973), *reh den* 414 U.S. 881.

290. *Roth v. United States* 354 U.S. 476 (1957).

291. *United States v. One Carton Positive Motion Picture Film Entitled "491"* 367 F 2d. 889 (2d Cir. 1966).

292. *United States v. 1,000 Copies of Magazines Entitled "Solis"* 254 F. Supp. 595 (DC Md 1966).

293. *People v. Richmond County News, Inc.* 9 NY 2d 578, 216 NYS 2d 369, 175 NE 2d 681 (ct. app. N.Y. 1961).

294. This deterrence is in the form of both court action prohibiting the dismissal of teachers and threats of court action by the teachers in question.

295. *See supra* note 177.

296. Ordinances prohibiting private employment discrimination against homosexuals include: Ann Arbor, Mich. Code Ch. 112, Secs. 9:151-9:155 (1972), Seattle, Wash. Ordinance 102,562 (Sept. 18, 1973); *See also, CIA Challenged for Denying Gays Security Clearance Could Set Precedent,* L.A. Daily J., Nov. 25, 1983 at 1, col. 2; Challenging homosexual discrimination in private employment: *DeSantis v. Pacific Telephone and Telegraph Co.* 608 F. 2d 327 (9th Cir. 1979).

297. Effective 1984, the Mormon Church stopped recording such information on its church records.

298. Los Angeles Times, March 11, 1984, Sec. I at 8, col. 1.

299. Address by Professor Dan F. Henderson, Univeristy of Washington School of Law (In Asia Series) Tokyo, Japan (April 5, 1983).

300. "And if any man will sue thee at law, and take away thy coat, let him have thy cloak also." Matthew 5:40.

301. Los Angeles Times, Feb. 16, 1984, Sec.I, at 1, col. 1.

302. *Id.* at 16, col. 1.

303. Leverett, *The Constitution and Federalism,* 24 Geo. Bar J. 352 (1962) [hereinafter cited as "Leverett"].

304. Merrill, *How to Lose a Federal Republic Without Even Half Trying,* 29 Okla. L. Rev. 577, 581 (1976).

305. *Id.*

306. Pub. L 93-643, 8114(a), 88 Stat 2286 (1975).

307. *Taylor v. Louisiana* 419 U.S. 522 (1975).

308. *Argeringer v. Hamlin* 407 U.S. 25 (1972).

309. 42 USC 1973 *et. seq.*

310. *Miranda v. Arizona* 384 U.S. 436 (1966).

311. *Mapp v. Ohio* 367 U.S. 643 (1961).

312. *See supra* notes 124 and 125 and accompanying text.

313. The retirement plan of the U.S. Armed Forces is but one example of this policy.

314. SYLVIA LAW, THE RIGHTS OF THE POOR 12-13 (1973).

315. *Fricke v. Lynch* 491 F. Supp. 381 (D.R.I. 1980).

316. Students of my generation were victims of this new approach to education which left us ill-prepared for the precision in calculation and communication that our society demands.

317. *Id*.

318. This position was explained to me by the son of an eminent Harvard Law School professor, himself a Harvard law student, who, no doubt, learned it from his environment.

319. MILTON & ROSE FRIEDMAN, FREE TO CHOOSE 190-191 (1980).

320. *Id*. at 191.

321. *Id*. at 190.

322. *Id*.

323. *Id*. at 191.

324. *Id*. at 192.

325. *See infra* note 348 and accompanying text.

326. *Id*.

327. Address by John C. Calhoun, in VIRGINIA COMMISSION ON CONSTITU-TIONAL GOVERNMENT, THE FORT HILL ADDRESS OF JOHN C. CALHOUN (1960).

328. *Fry v. United States* 421 U.S. 542, 559 (1975) (Rehnquist,J., dissenting).

329. Gladstone, *Kin Beyond the Sea*, North American Rev., Sept. 1878.

330. This period is calculated from 1776, including the events of the Continential Congress under the Articles of Confederation, to 1788 when the call for constitutional revision was issued.

331. Leverett, *supra* note 303 at 352.

332. *Id*.

333. 92 U.S. 542 (1876).

334. 247 U.S. 251, 275-276 (1918).

335. U.S. Const. art. I, Sec. 8.

336. *Id.* art II, Sec. 3.

337. *Id.* art II, sec. 2.

338. Leverett, *supra* note 303 at 353.

339. B. SCHWARTZ, THE LAW IN AMERICA 47 (1974).

340. Merrill, *supra* note 304 at 579.

341. Leverett, *supra* note 303 at 353.

342. U.S. Const. amend. x

343. Mason, *Must We Continue the States'Rights Debate?*, 18 Rutgers L. Rev. 60, 61 (1963).

344. *Id.* at 60.

345. Prof. Charles L. Black, Jr., Professor of Jurisprudence, Yale Law School, Cong. Rec. 8263 (daily ed., May 15, 1963), as quoted in McGovern, *Confederation vs. Union*, 9 S.D.L. Rev. 1 (1964).

346. Kilpatrick, *The Case for States' Rights*, in A NATION OF STATES 95 (R.A. Goldwin ed. 1963) at 88.

347. *Id.* at 89.

348. Merrill, *supra* note 304 at 584.

349. Douglas, *The Tenth Amendment: The Foundation of Liberty*, 16 New Hampshire Bar J. 286 (1975).

350. 421 U.S. 515, 542 (1975).

351. Mason, *supra* note 343 at 60.

352. STATE GOVERNMENT 10 (Winter, 1963).

353. J. FRANK, LAW AND THE MODERN MIND 102 (1930).

354. Merrill, *supra* note 304 at 587.

355. M. THOMAS, FELIX FRANKFURTER, SCHOLAR ON THE BENCH 286 (1960).

356. Heldt, *The Tenth Amendment Iceberg*, 30 Hastings L. J. 1763, 1764 (1979).

357. Leverett, *supra* note 303 at 358.

358. *Id.* at 355.

359. *Id.* at 354-355 (footnotes omitted).

360. *Worcester v. Georgia* 6 Peters 515 (1832); *Brown v. Epps* 91 Va. 726, 21 SE 114 (Va. 1895).

361. Douglas, *supra* note 349 at 293.

362. Choper, *The Scope of National Power Vis-A-Vis the States: The Dispensability of Judicial Review*, 86 Yale L.J. 1552 (1977).

363. *Id.* at 1553.

364. Cowen, *Some Additional Thoughts on "States' Rights"*, 39 St. Johns L. Rev. 288, 290 (1965).

365. Leverett, *supra* note 303 at 362.

366. The Japanese, for example, often call Anglo-Saxons the "real Americans."

367. The Constitution was drafted "to secure the blessings of liberty to...our posterity." (U.S. Const. preamble).

368. "Contrary to widely broadcast statements of 'popular' American historians and even some serious and scholarly chronicles of our national records, a very considerable proportion of early settlers in New England were university graduates. Puritanism was in the main a revolt of the mind from the fixed confines of thought in the Anglican church establishment and hence, many men of intellect were drawn into the movement." (PAUL FRANKLIN JOHNSON, CAPTAIN JOHN JOHNSON GENEALOGY 416 (1951).

369. "Behold, I will send you Elijah the prophet before the coming of the great and dreadful day of the Lord: And he shall turn the heart of the fathers to the children, and the heart of the children to their fathers, lest I come and smite the earth with a curse." (Malachi 4:6).

370. *See supra* note 244 and accompanying text.

371. "'Race' is the witchcraft of our time . . . It is the contemporary myth. Man's most dangerous myth." (A. MONTAGU, MAN'S MOST DANGEROUS MYTH: THE FALLACY OF RACE 23 (1964).

372. Fair Housing Act, 42 USCS Sec. 3604 (a)—(e); P.L. 90-284, April 11, 1968, 82 Stat 83, Sec. 804.

373. 42 USCS Secs. 2000c—2000c-9; Titles IV, VI and VIII Civil Rights Act of 1964, P.L. 88-352 July 2, 1964, 78 Stat 241, 252.

374. Title VII of Civil Rights Act of 1964 Sec. 703(a); 42 USCS Sec. 2000e-2(a).

375. *Loving v. Virginia* 388 U.S. 1, 87 S Ct. 1817 (1967).

376. In 1969, University of California, Berkeley, professor, Arthur Jensen published an article in *Harvard Educational Review* suggesting that genetic factors affect Negro-white intelligence differences (Jensen, *How Much can We Boost IQ and Scholastic Achievement?* 39 Harv. Educ. Rev. 1 (1969). Attempts were made by groups calling him racist to have him fired, to invade his classes and to harass his research assistant (Delgado, Bradley, Bunkenroad, Chavez, Doering, Lardiere, Reeves, Smith and Windhausen, *Can Science Be Inopportune? Constitutional Validity of Governmental Restrictions on Race-IQ Research,* 31 UCLA L. Rev. 130, 137 (1983).

377. See text at note 387 *infra.*

378. Webster's New World Dictionary, 2d ed., *s.v.* "race."

379. Jacquard, *Myths Under the Microscope,* UNESCO Courier, Nov. 1983 at 19.

380. *See, e.g.* U.S. Bureau of the Census tables in NEWSPAPER ENTERPRISE ASSOCIATION, INC., THE WORLD ALMANAC & BOOK OF FACTS 1984 at 203.

381. Webster's New World Dictionary, 2d ed., *s.v.* "Caucasoid."

382. *Id.*

383. But see *In Re Ahmed Hassan* 48 F. Supp. 843, 845 (Dist.Ct., E.D. Mich. 1942) which suggests that no persons of Asiatic stock, particularly those from the Mohammedan world, could be considered "white persons" within the meaning of the then existing statute.

384. *See supra* note 11 and accompanying text.

385. "To sum up," says Professor Montagu, "the indictment against the anthropological conception of race is (1) that it is artificial; (2) that it does not agree with the facts; (3) that it leads to confusion and the perpetuation of error, and, finally, that for all these reasons, it is meaningless" (A. MONTAGU. RACE. SCIENCE AND HUMANITY 8 (1963).

386. *Id.*

387. 20 UN Chronicle, Oct. 1983 at 54.

388. Retamar, *Mixed Metamorphosis,* UNESCO Courier, Nov. 1983 at 22.

389. Richardson, *Racism: A Tort of Outrage,* 61 Or. L. Rev. 267 (1982).

390. 20 UN Chronicle, Oct. 1983 at 41.

391. Brown, *Racists Are Made, Not Born,* PARENTS, Apr. 1983 at 42.

392. Webster's Third New International Dictionary *s.v.* "racism."

393. Memmi, *'Us' and 'Them',* UNESCO Courier, Nov. 1983 at 11.

394. *See e.g.* Jacquard, *Myths Under the Microsocpe*, UNESCO Courier, Nov. 1983 at 17.

395. Memmi, *supra* note 393.

396. Retamer, *Mixed Metamorphosis*, UNESCO Courier, Nov. 1983 at 21.

397. *See* Memmi, *supra* note 393 at 12.

398. Andrew Jackson thought the Indians were nothing more than simple savages (WARD, ANDREW JACKSON, SYMBOL FOR AN AGE 40-41 (1974). And Abraham Lincoln said to a group of Negro delegates in Washington D.C.: "Even when you cease to be slaves, you are yet far removed from being placed on an equality with white people . . . I cannot alter it if I would . . . "(Pittman, *All Men Are Not Equal*, 17 Ala. Law. 252, 259 (1956). Theodore Roosevelt believed in white superiority and supported eugenics (Delgado, *et al. supra* note 376 at 202, note 446). In 1924, Congress passed the Johnson Restriction Act which imposed "national origin quotas" based partially on data which "proved" that Mediterranean races and Negroes were inferior. (*Id.* at 202-203).

399. MONTAGU, RACE, SCIENCE AND HUMANITY 8 (1963).

400. "There is nothing to prove that biological superiority, assuming that it exists, leads to psychological or cultural superiority." (Memmi, *supra* note 393 at 11.) "Earlier in the [1960s] decade, as the condition of blacks became a national issue, Piaget's views on the role of experience in intellectual growth [as opposed to factors of heredity] had gained favor . . . "(Delgado, *et al supra* note 376 at 136-137).

401. *See, Id.* at 194-195.

402. *Id.*

403. F. D. SCOTT, WORLD MIGRATION IN MODERN TIMES 168 (1968).

404. Webster's New World Dictionary, 2d ed. *s.v.* "Central America," "North America," "South America."

405. *see* text accompanying note 12 *supra*.

406. ANDERSON, IMMIGRATION 8 (1981).

407. I Stat. 103 (1790); Gordon, *The Racial Barrier to American Citizenship*, 93 U. Pa. L. Rev. 237, 238 (1945).

408. Gordon, *supra* note 407 at 238.

409. 60 U.S. (19 How.) 393 at 407 (1857).

410. Wright, *Bangs and Whimpers XXXIX: The Legacy of Dred Scott*, 5 N.C.L. Rev. 148, 150 (1974).

411. 16 Stat. 250 (1870); Gordon, *supra* note 407 at 239.

412. 22 Stat. 58, 61 (1882); Gordon, *supra* 407 at 239.

413. Gordon, *supra* note 407 at 237.

414. *Ozawa v. United States* 260 U.S. 178, 43 Sup. Ct. 65 (1922).

415. *United States v. Thind* 262 U.S. 204, 209 (1923).

416. *In re Din* 27 F.2d 568 (N.D. Cal. 1928).

417. *Wadia v. United States* 101 F. 2d 7 (C.C.A. 2d, 1939).

418. *In re Hassan* 48 F. Supp. 843 (E.D. Mich. 1942).

419. *United States v. Thind* 261 U.S. 204, 213 (1923).

420. The quoted explanation is a composite analysis obtained from discussions with various foreign businessmen and attorneys.

421. Pitman, *All Men Are Not Equal*, 17 Ala. Law. 252, 259 (1956).

422. *United States v. Thind* 261 U.S. 204, 215 (1923).

423. Jones, *I Speak for the White Race*, 18 Ala. Law. 201 (1957).

424. USA Today, Oct. 16, 1984, Sec. I, at 1, col. 2.

425. *See* TIME, May 7, 1984 at 32.

426. For a brief discussion of the Jim Crow laws that denied Negro citizenship rights afforded whites, see WOODWARD, THE STRANGE CAREER OF JIM CROW (1957).

427. 60 U.S. (19 How.) 393 (1857).

428. *Furman v. Georgia*, 408 U.S. 238 (1972); *see also* Comment, *Constitutional Law: The Death Penalty: A Critique of the Philosophical Bases Held to Satisfy the Eighth Amendment Requirements for its Justification*, 34 Okla. L. Rev. 567 (1981).

429. *Holt v. Sarver* 309 F. Supp. 362 (E. D. Ark., 1970); *see also* Comment, *Unconstitutional Prison Conditions as a Ground for Habeas Corpus Relief in Extradition Proceedings*, 49 UMKC L. Rev. 64 (1980).

430. *Roe v. Wade* 410 U.S. 113 (1973).

431. *Engel v. Vitale* 370 U.S. 421 (1962).

432. *See*: Steward, *Taking Christ out of Christmas?* 69 A.B.A.J., Dec. 1983 at 1835.

433. *See: Eisenstadt v. Baird* 405 U.S. 438 (1972) where the court held that a bar on the distribution of contraceptives to unmarried persons is unconstitutional; *Norton v. Macy* 417 F. 2d 1161 (D.C. Cir. 1969) where a state university was forced to hire as a librarian a male homosexual who tried to marry his male sex partner.

434. For example, a federal judge struck down a Utah state cable television obscenity law banning pornography via television in the state. L.A. Daily J., Jan. 15, 1982, Sec. 1 at 5, col. 4.

435. *See e.g., Graham v. Richardson* 403 U.S. 365 (1971).

436. *Brown v. Board of Education* 347 U.S. 483 (1954).

437. Palmer, *The Fourteenth Amendment: Some Reflections on Segregation in Schools*, 49 A.B.A.J. 637, 645 (July 1963).

438. Shanahan, *Proposed Constitutional Amendments: They Will Strengthen Federal-State Relations*, 49 A.B.A.J. 631 (July 1963).

439. U.S. Const., amend. XIV.

440. Senate Resolution No. 39 (Res. Act No. 45) of the 1957 regular session of the Georgia General Assembly, passed March 8, 1957. *See also The Maryland Petition Committee, etc. et al. v. Lyndon B. Johnson, etc., et al.* 265 F. Supp. 823 (1967) which was an action in Federal Court against the President of the United States seeking declaratory judgment that the 14th and 15th amendments are null and void.

441. U.S. Const. amend. XV.

442. *See, e.g. Gitlow v. New York* 268 U.S. 652 (1925); *Mapp v. Ohio* 367 U.S. 643 (1961).

443. The South Carolina Act of February 14, 1956, Calendar No. S.514.

444. House Concurrent Resolution No. 5 of the second 1957 special session of the Texas Legislature.

445. Comment, *An Affirmative Constitutional Right: The Tenth Amendment and the Resolution of Federalism Conflicts*, 13 San Diego L. Rev. 876, 878 (1976); 3 J. Elliot, Debates on the Federal Constitution 608 (1836).

446. Comment, *Id.* at 878-879.

447. *See: Legal Definition of Race*, 3 Race Rel. L. Rep. 571 (June 1958).

448. *Id.*

449. *Id.* at 573.

450. *Id.* at 574.

451. *Id.* at 579.

452. *See supra* note 398.

453. *Johnson v. Board of Education* 166 N.C. 468, 82 S.E. 832 (1914); *see also Mullin v. Belcher* 142 Ky 312, 134 S.W. 1151, 1152 (1911); *Van Camp v. Board of Education* 9 Ohio St. 406, 411 (1859).

454. *Legal Definition of Race, supra* note 447 at 574; Va Code Ann. Secs. 20-54 (Michie, 1950).

455. *See* Va Code Ann. Secs 1-14 (Michie, 1956, Supp); *Legal Definition of Race, Id.*

456. 307 U.S. 433 (1939).

457. Comment, *Proposed Legislation on the Convention Method of Amending the United States Constitution*, 85 Harv.L.Rev. 1612 (1972).

458. The U.S. Supreme Court has held in a series of cases that the equal protection clause of the fourteenth amendment requires that each house of a state legislature be apportioned by population. *See, e.g., Lucas v. Forty-Fourth General Assembly* 377 U.S. 713 (1964); *Reynolds v. Sims* 372 U.S. 533 (1964).

459. Harv. L. Rev. Comment, *supra* note 457 at 1618.

460. *Id.*

461. *See Hearings on S. 2307 Before the Subcommittee on Separation of Powers of the Senate Committee on the Judiciary*, 90th Cong., 1st Sess. 23, 38-39 (1967) (remarks of Senator Proxmire and Mr. Sorensen).

462. S 2307, 90th Cong., 1st Sess. (1967) [hereinafter "Ervin Bill"]; S2812 98th Cong. 1st Sess. (1984) [hereinafter "Helms Bill"].

463. Helms Bill 9 (c).

464. Note, *The Constitutional Convention, Its Nature and Powers—And the Amending Procedure*, 1966 Utah L. Rev. 390, 392 (1966).

465. *Id.*

466. *Id.*

467. Harv. L. Rev. Comment, *supra* note 457 at 1612.

468. Comment, *Good Intentions, New Inventions, and Article V Constitutional Conventions*, 58 Tex. L. Rev. 131 (1979).

469. THE FEDERALIST No. 43 at 274-275 (J. Madison) (H. Lodge ed. 1923).

470. 1 J. BURGESS, POLITICAL SCIENCE AND COMPARATIVE CONSTITUTIONAL LAW 137 (1893) *as cited in* Tex. L. Rev. *supra* note 468 at 136-137.

471. Tex. L. Rev. Comment *Id*. at 136-137.

472. Gunther, *The Convention Method of Amending the United States Constitution*, 14 Ga. L. Rev. 1, 5 (1979).

473. 16 Am. Jur. 2d, Constitutional Law Sec. 21 (1979).

474. Tex. L. Rev. Comment *supra* note 468 at 138.

475. *Cited in*: Van Alstyne, *Does Article V Restrict the States to Calling Unlimited Conventions Only?—A Letter to a Colleague*, 1978 Duke L. J. 1290, 1296 (1978).

476. *See e.g.* Black, *Amending the Constitution: A Letter to a Congressman*, 82 Yale L. J. 199 (1972).

477. Tex. L. Rev. *supra* note 468 at 138, *citing* ABA SPECIAL CONSTITUTIONAL CONVENTION STUDY COMM., AMENDMENT OF THE CONSTITUTION BY THE CONVENTION METHOD UNDER ARTICLE V, at 59-61 (1974).

478. Harv. L. Rev. Comment *supra* note 457 at 1614.

479. *Id*.

480. Helms Bill 6 (a); Ervin Bill 6 (a).

481. S. Rep. No. 336, 92d Cong. 1st Sess. 9 (1971), *cited in* Harv. L. Rev. Comment *supra* note 457 at 1628.

482 Tex. L. Rev. Comment *supra* note 468 at 138 (footnote omitted).

483. *Id*. at 140.

484. 253 U.S. 221 (1920).

485. *Id*. at 229.

486. *Id*. at 227.

487. Ervin Bill Sec. 3 (a), Helms Bill Sec. 3 (a).

488. Black *supra* note 476 at 210.

489. *Id*.

490. *Id*.

491. This is the position taken by American Jurisprudence 16 Am. Jur. 2d Constitutional Law Sec. 21 (1979).

492. Tex. L. Rev. Comment *supra* note 468 at 137 (footnotes omitted).

493. *See* S. Rep. *supra* note 481 at 11; 117 Cong. Rec. 516, 525 (daily ed. Oct. 19, 1971); 96 Cong. 1st Sess. S 520 Sec. 5 (a); Harv. L. Rev. Comment *supra* note 457 at 1619.

494. Ervin Bill, Sec. 5 (b); Helms Bill, Sec. 5 (b).

495. Tex. L. Rev. Comment *supra* note 468 at 138, *citing ABA supra* note 478 at 59-61.

496. 16 Am. Jur. 2d Constitutional Law Sec. 21 (1979).

497. Harv. L. Rev. Comment *supra* note 457 at 1635 (footnotes omitted).

498. Ervin Bill, Secs. 3 (b), 5 (c), 13 (c); Helms Bill Secs. 3(b), 5 (c), 13 (c).

499. Black, *supra* note 476 at 210-211.

500. Tex. L. Rev. Comment *supra* note 468 at 139.

501. U.S. Const. art. I, Sec. 7.

502. S. Rep. No. 92-336, 92 Cong. 1st Sess. 12-13 (1971).

503. *Id*.

504. 3 U.S. (3 Dall.) 378 (1798).

505. *Id*. at 380 n. (a).

506. 253 U.S. 221, 229 (1920).

507. Black, *supra* note 476 at 206.

508. *Id*. at 208.

509. Harv. L. Rev. Comment, *supra* note 457 at 1622 (footnotes omitted).

510. *Id*. at 1623.

511. S. 1710, 96th Cong., 1st Sess. (1979).

512. Ervin Bill, Sec. 7(a); Helms Bill, Sec. 7(a).

513. Ervin Bill Sec. 7(a).

514. F. A. MAGRUDER, AMERICAN GOVERNMENT IN 1921 at 31 (1921).

515. Harv. L. Rev. Comment, *supra* note 457 at 1618.

516. U.S. Const. art I, Sec. 8.

517. *See: McCulloch v. Maryland* 17 U.S. (4 Wheat) 316 (1819); Harv. L. Rev. Comment, *supra* note 457 at 1617.

518. Harv. L. Rev. Comment, *supra* note 457 at 1617 n. 26.

519. Gunther, *supra* note 472 at 23-24 (footnotes omitted).

520. Ervin Bill Sec. 7(a).

521. F. A. MAGRUDER, *supra* note 514 at 134.

522. Harv. L. Rev. Comment, *supra* note 457 at 1625.

523. Black, *supra* note 476 at 204.

524. Helms Bill Sec. 10 (a); Ervin Bill Sec. 10 (a).

525. Harv. L. Rev. Comment, *supra* note 457 at 1633, n. 106.

526. *Id.* at 1633 (footnotes omitted).

527. U.S. Const. art V.

528. Tex. L. Rev. Comment, *supra* note 468 at 141.

The notes contained in this book are in accord with the style set forth in *A Uniform System of Citation*, 13th ed., published by the Harvard Law Review Association, and, where applicable, *A Manual of Style*, 13th ed., published by the University of Chicago Press, except for the following:

1. legal and other professional periodicals, dictionaries, and encyclopedias are cited in ordinary Roman type rather than large and small capitals;

2. periodicals of general circulation are cited in all capitals; and

3. books and pamphlets are cited in all capitals rather than in large and small capitals.

# SUBJECT MATTER INDEX

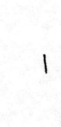